*A Fireside Book*

PUBLISHED BY SIMON & SCHUSTER

*New York London Toronto Sydney Tokyo Singapore*

# The Miracle Nutrient Cookbook

*100 Delicious*

*Antioxidant-Enriched*

*Recipes and*

*Menu Suggestions*

*for Optimum Health*

TAMARA HOLT AND
MAUREEN CALLAHAN, M.S., R.D.

*A Lynn Sonberg Book*

**F**

*FIRESIDE*
*Rockefeller Center*
*1230 Avenue of the Americas*
*New York, NY 10020*

*Copyright © 1995 by Lynn Sonberg Book Services*
*All rights reserved,*
*including the right of reproduction*
*in whole or in part in any form.*

*FIRESIDE and colophon are registered*
*trademarks of Simon & Schuster Inc.*

*Research about human nutrition and the health effects of antioxidants and other*
*nutrients is constantly evolving. Although we have made every effort to include the most accurate*
*and up-to-date information in this book, what we know about this complex subject may change*
*with time. Readers should consult a qualified health professional about any health or*
*medical issues, and before making any major dietary changes.*

*Designed by Barbara M. Bachman*
*Illustrations by Amy Bryant*

*Manufactured in the United States of America*

*10   9   8   7   6   5   4   3   2   1*

*Library of Congress Cataloging-in-Publication Data*

*Holt, Tamara.*
    *The miracle nutrient cookbook : 100 delicious antioxidant-enriched recipes and menu*
    *suggestions for optimum health / by Tamara Holt & Maureen Callahan.*
        *p. cm.*
    *"A Lynn Sonberg book."*
    *"A Fireside book."*
    *1. Nutrition. 2. Antioxidants. 3. Free radicals (Chemistry)—Pathophysiology.*
    *4. Health. I. Callahan, Maureen. II. Title.*
    *RA784.H596   1995*
    *613.2'6—dc20            95-3830                         CIP*

*ISBN 0-684-80238-4*

# Contents

## 5.  *Breakfast Foods and Drinks*  •  *61*

## 6.  *Soups*  •  *77*

## 7.  *Vegetable Main Dishes*  •  *93*

## 8. *Meat, Fish, and Poultry Main Dishes* • *117*

## 9. *Main-Dish Salads* • *141*

## 10. *Side Dishes* • *157*

## 11. *Side Salads* • *175*

# Introduction

If you picked up this book, chances are you are one of the millions of Americans who are excited by the growing body of research that tells us that the food we eat can dramatically affect our health . . . not just whether or not we'll get a particular disease, but also the very quality and even length of our lives.

As you'll see, many scientists believe that antioxidants and certain other disease-fighting chemicals in food are the key both to optimum health and maximum lifespan. With this book as your guide, incorporating these powerful nutrients in your diet has never been simpler—or more delicious.

First, nutrition expert Maureen Callahan provides an overview of the scientific evidence; what exactly do we know about the healing and/or protective power of antioxidants? Then she translates that knowledge into practical, everyday strategies for meal planning as well as shopping for and storing the best foods for an antioxidant-rich diet. For instance, did you know that produce left at room temperature for one day may lose as much as 30 to 40 percent of its vitamin C content? Or did you realize that simply eating one raw carrot per day might be enough to dramatically reduce your risk of having a heart attack or stroke?

Indeed, whether your concern is reducing the risk of cancer and heart disease, boosting your immune power, or increasing longevity, antioxidants are the key.

What's more, if you follow the eating plan and recipes in this book and consume your antioxidants within the context of a low-fat diet, any excess pounds you've been carrying should gradually melt away.

Finally, sample menus and one hundred mouth-watering recipes developed by Tamara Holt (analyzed for calories and ten important nutrients) will allow you to feast on such delicacies as Tomato-stuffed Pork Tenderloin with Roasted Poblano Sauce or Braised Chicken with Apricots and Ginger, all the while boosting your intake of key nutrients that could help lengthen your lifespan and improve your health. Imagine indulging in desserts like Carrot Spice Cake or Pumpkin Pie, which pack huge quantities of the powerful antioxidant beta-carotene yet are low in fat and rich in flavor. From Molasses-Nut Granola to Moroccan Lamb and Vegetable Stew to Italian Seafood Salad, the wide variety of recipes in this book will help introduce you and your family to a new way of eating . . . and a new way of living: *The Miracle Nutrient Cookbook.*

## Chapter 1

# Antioxidants: Nutritional Powerhouses

While scientists have yet to find any kind of magic antiaging elixir, there is rapidly accumulating evidence that diet could play a role in turning back the aging clock. Scientists pinpoint antioxidants like beta-carotene, vitamin C, vitamin E, and the trace mineral selenium as the most potent dietary antiaging compounds. Speculation is that these substances exert a strong influence over the aging process by squelching damaging substances in the body called free radicals, substances believed to advance aging and promote disease.

Keep in mind that the whole business of antioxidants as well as their impact on aging is relatively new scientific territory, and it's too soon for scientists to make any firm promises. Yet one thing is clear from the research: Antioxidants and other disease-fighting chemicals in foods (indoles in cruciferous vegetables, sulforophane in broccoli, and flavonoids in apples) appear capable of helping to stave off or prevent some of the damage that leads to aging. Perhaps just as critical, these substances seem to bolster the immune system, the body's warrior against illness.

As well as being nutritional powerhouses, antioxidants may also reduce your risk for dozens of diseases, including heart disease and cancer, the top two killers in the United States. Preliminary reports also suggest a protective role for antioxidants in a number of other chronic ills, including everything from Alzheimer's to cataracts to osteoarthritis to cystic fibrosis. Indeed, when it comes to aging, scientists no longer believe that a lengthy lifespan is solely due to genetics or advanced medical technology. Free radicals and antioxidant-rich foods are a big part of the aging picture.

In the course of normal metabolism your body produces compounds called free radicals, damaging substances that can wreak havoc on both individual cells and whole body systems. These same free radicals can also be encountered and absorbed from the environment through compounds such as ozone, cigarette smoke, and polluted air. To understand how free radicals can disrupt and tamper with your body requires some understanding regarding their chemical nature.

To the chemist, the term "free radical" refers to any atom or group of atoms with an unpaired electron. If you can remember back to Chemistry 101, an atom that lacks an electron is unstable, or "highly reactive." In order to become more stable, the free radical searches out an electron to pair with, typically attacking cell membranes and tissues that can unleash an electron. Once that electron is salvaged, the free radical stabilizes. But in the wake of its stabilization effort that radical leaves another substance without an electron, and another, setting off a chain of free-radical reactions.

Fortunately, the body produces enzymes and compounds that can squelch free radicals. In addition, antioxidants in the diet—vitamin C, vitamin E, beta-carotene, selenium—can hook up with and inactivate free radicals and thereby prevent these treacherous compounds from harming the body. Of course, sometimes a heavy onslaught of free-radical reactions overwhelms the body's defense system. In fact, a growing number of studies implicate free-radical damage in the cause and development of numerous diseases, including the top two killers: cancer and heart disease. Here is a rundown of how researchers theorize that free radicals create damage and how this damage might result in illness.

### FREE RADICALS

- can break and tear DNA (genetic material), causing mutations or changes that could pave the way to cancer.

- can cause serious damage to parts of the eye (retina, lens), setting the stage for cataracts and macular degeneration.

- can convert or alter harmful LDL cholesterol, turning it into a form that sticks more readily to artery walls and that can eventually build up and clog those blood vessels.

Free radicals may also play a role in essential hypertension, Alzheimer's, immune deficiency, osteoarthritis, Parkinson's disease, insulin dependent diabetes mellitus, preeclampsia, Huntington's chorea, and a few rare genetic disorders. Despite the fact that most of these free radical-disease connections are based on speculation and theory, researchers have definite ideas on how the substances in question might contribute to accelerating aging, impairing the immune system, and provoking disease.

## Free Radicals and Aging

It wasn't until the middle 1950s that scientists began to theorize that free radicals played a role in aging. Belief was that there might be just one single cause of aging, one that could be modified by either genetic or environmental factors. That cause, researchers theorized, might be free-radical reactions within the body. These reactions were believed to cause damage that could speed up the process of aging as well as the development of chronic diseases like heart disease and cancer.

One of the first ways that scientists began to test this theory was through diet. Since antioxidant substances can bind and immobilize free radicals, researchers wondered if dietary changes designed to reduce the number of free-radical reactions could increase the life span. In the early seventies came animal studies that found that dietary measures designed to cut back on free-radical reactions appeared to increase average life expectancy by as much as 20 to 30 percent. Dietary ingredients suspected of helping to limit free-radical damage included nutrients that act as antioxidants, such as vitamin E, vitamin C, beta-carotene, and selenium. Newer, more recent findings are uncovering a whole host of other substances in foods (flavonoids, indoles, and glutathione) that may also protect against free-radical damage.

Bear in mind that none of these findings is yet considered a medical certainty. But with many studies supporting the fact that cellular aging may be related to a decreased capacity of the system to inactivate free radicals, it seems logical that dietary antioxidants could play a role in delaying or retarding the aging process. Key to this theory is the role antioxidant nutrients play in the health of the immune system.

## Free Radicals and Immune Function

While antioxidants destroy damaging free radicals throughout the body, their role in immune health seems to involve much more. Studies confirm that several dietary antioxidants actually help to boost immune defenses. Acting as critical cofactors, they galvanize various immune-defense warriors, turning them on and off in response to the foreign invaders that cause illness. For example, beta-carotene helps to activate natural killer (NK) cells, immune fighters that identify and eradicate viruses and tumors. Vitamin E appears to help rejuvenate certain responses in the aging immune system; vitamin C boosts others. Minerals like selenium and zinc (not an antioxidant but critical to healthy immune function) also seem important.

Currently, researchers are trying to determine the precise amounts of each of these substances that are beneficial to immune health. Most of the work to date has been done in the lab or with animals. But preliminary studies with people are beginning to show promise. In one report, researchers who gave beta-carotene supplements (180 milligrams per day) to people with HIV discovered that the antioxidant triggered increased "helper" T lymphocyte activity. T lymphocytes, if you remember, are white blood cells that are either "killers" or "helpers" when it comes to identifying and mounting a defense against infections and tumors.

Another study suggests that adequate beta-carotene in the diet can prevent ultraviolet (UV-A) radiation from damaging immune function.

In a Canadian research project, scientists found that seniors taking a daily multivitamin (with extra doses of antioxidants beta-carotene and vitamin E) tablet for one year were less likely to become sick and were easier to treat than their cohorts who relied on a placebo. Perhaps even better news, the supplement users, when they did get sick, suffered with symptoms for only half as long as the placebo group. That makes sense, considering that a weakened immune system can mean it's difficult to fight off both minor ailments such as the common cold and major ailments such as heart disease and cancer.

## Free Radicals and Cancer

In order for cancer to develop, initiators or promoting substances (carcinogens) must be present. Some experts think it's possible that free-radical reactions may serve as a continuous source of some of these initiators and promoters. Speculation is that free radicals may weaken and damage DNA and thereby allow for adaptations that encourage the growth of cancer. In addition, bear in mind that many cancers occur later in life. That could be tied, at least in part, to the fact that the number of free-radical reactions in the body appears to increase with age. At the same time, an older body's aging immune system is going to be weaker and less able to fight off foreign invaders.

Early reports indicate that diets rich in fruits and vegetables, possibly due to antioxidants and other cancer-fighting chemicals (phytochemicals) in foods, may lower cancer risk. A recent review of these studies shows that 132 different research projects find a link between specific foods or the antioxidants they contain and a lower risk for cancer at 15 different body sites. Some of the strongest evidence to date outlines a connection between beta-carotene and lung cancer risk. In one early study, a group of Chicago researchers looked at the health outcomes of a group of men and noticed that those in the group who ate very few beta-carotene-rich foods were more likely to die in later years from lung cancer.

However, compelling as the evidence is that supports the cancer-protective ability of beta-carotene, it is not the final word. A recent clinical trial not only questions how beneficial beta-carotene is as a protector against cancer, but also questions the safety of beta-carotene supplements. When Finnish researchers studied a group of men taking supplements of 20 milligrams of beta-carotene per day, they found that these men had an 18 percent higher risk for lung cancer than men not taking supplements.

Recommendations about the use of beta-carotene supplements seem up in the air as scientists try to figure out what this preliminary and unusual finding means. In the meantime, researchers have no qualms about the beta-carotene found in foods. More important, they point out that people who eat plenty of fruits and vegetables, the kinds of foods in which beta-carotene is found, do have a lower risk for many types of cancer.

In addition, fifteen separate research studies find that vitamin C may offer some protection against both stomach and esophageal cancers. Numerous other researchers have connected high vitamin C intakes with a lower risk for cancer of the lung, larynx, colon, rectum, pancreas, cervix, and bladder. It's difficult for researchers to pinpoint the precise ingredients in fruits, vegetables, and antioxidant-rich foods that confer protection. Yet the National Cancer Institute is promoting "5 a Day" as a guideline for the number of fruit and vegetable servings needed as part of any basic anticancer diet strategy. These experts conclude that a diet rich in fruits, vegetables, and whole grains is valuable as a hedge not only against cancer, but against such other ailments as high blood pressure, heart disease, and cataracts.

## Free Radicals and Cataracts

Cataracts result from changes in the delicate protein fibers found in the lens of the eye. These changes cause the lens to become more opaque and vision to become clouded. Theory has it that cataracts may be the result of free-radical damage (oxidative changes) that occurs due to a lifetime of exposure to the sun's ultraviolet rays. That's why it comes as no surprise that researchers are finding that antioxidant-rich fruits and vegetables may help delay or prevent cataract formation. In Boston, in studies at the Department of Agriculture's Human Nutrition Research Center on Aging, scientists found that people who eat less than one and a half servings of fruits and vegetables per day are six times more likely to develop cataracts than people who eat generous amounts—three and a half servings daily—of fruits and vegetables. (If you consider recent surveys that find most Americans are lucky if they eat one serving of produce per day, it would seem likely that the number of Americans who develop cataracts may dramatically increase in the not-so-distant future.)

These same scientists also documented an increased risk for cataracts in people with low blood levels of two antioxidant nutrients: vitamin C and beta-carotene. The beta-carotene finding goes along with a British study that found diets rich in fruits and vegetables containing beta-carotene seemed to help protect against cataracts. Women in the study who ate the highest levels of beta-carotene–rich foods had a 40 percent lower risk of cataracts. Also on the list of potential protectors against cataracts is the most powerful of the antioxidant nutrients, vitamin E. Studies conducted at the Wilmer Eye Institute in Baltimore suggest that high blood levels of vitamin E protect not only against cataracts but the more serious eye disease, macular degeneration, which is a painless but progressive illness that damages the retina of older adults. Loss of vision is gradual and can eventually lead to blindness.

## Free Radicals and Heart Disease

Cutting back on fat and cholesterol, keeping active, and controlling blood pressure are all undoubtedly critical strategies for lowering heart-disease risk. Yet the most intriguing new area of heart-disease research doesn't single out any of these dietary and lifestyle components. Instead, it focuses on the role three of the antioxidant nutrients—vitamin E, vitamin C, and beta-carotene—may play in staving off the nation's number one killer.

The most recent reports suggest a powerful role for vitamin E in warding off heart disease. In two separate studies from researchers at Harvard Medical School—one done with men and one with women—participants taking vitamin E supplements were at much less risk for heart disease than volunteers who had very low vitamin E intakes. In addition, studies find that beta-carotene–rich foods like carrots, pumpkin, and spinach also seem to offer protection against cardiovascular disease. One study from Harvard Medical School found that women who ate 15 milligrams of beta-carotene per day (the amount found in one large carrot) had a 22 percent lower risk of heart attack and a 40 percent lower risk of stroke than women who ate far less. The Physicians' Health Study, a large project aimed at studying the impact of aspirin on heart disease and beta-carotene on cancer risk among doctors, surprised researchers by showing that beta-carotene had an influence on heart-disease risk. Doctors in the group who were already showing signs of heart disease ended up cutting their risk of heart attack and stroke almost in half with a dose of 50 milligrams of beta-carotene every other day.

Although its role is not so direct, vitamin C may also impact on heart disease risk. In studies at Tufts University in Boston, scientists noticed lower blood-pressure readings in people whose diets were rich in foods containing vitamin C. These same folks also had higher levels of HDL, the so-called good cholesterol that carries cholesterol away from arteries, than people who ate very little citrus, broccoli, or other produce rich in vitamin C. Speculation is that some of the protection against heart disease conferred by antioxidants is due to their ability to prevent free radicals from worsening the impact of LDL, or what is commonly referred to as the "bad" cholesterol. As explained earlier, if free radicals oxidize LDL (to obtain the electron they are missing), the LDL will be altered. The problem is that this altered form of LDL is stickier, and so more likely to adhere to artery walls and clog them.

## Free Radicals and Alzheimer's

Scientists are far from certain about the underlying cause of Alzheimer's, but numerous theories abound. Some tie the cause of this debilitating progressive disease, which is the most common type of senile dementia, to everything from chronic infection to aluminum poisoning to free-radical damage. That last theory seems quite promising. It's based on the hypothesis that mutations or changes in DNA mitochondria, the powerhouse of the cell, can cause nerve cells in the brain to degenerate. (Some amount of cell damage and death is due to the normal aging process of these nerve cells. But with Alzheimer's the process appears to be highly accelerated.) If this proves to be the case, it might some day be possible to shut down or at least diminish the level of free-radical reactions that lead to Alzheimer's with a diet rich in antioxidants.

Far too little is understood about Alzheimer's to warrant the prescription of an antioxidant-rich diet as a cure. But since these nutrients appear to help stave off the two major killers—heart disease and cancer—that's already reason enough to include them in the diet.

## Some Other Ailments, Common and Uncommon

While the mechanism is far from clear, preliminary reports hint that antioxidants could have an impact on preventing the development of essential hypertension, osteoarthritis, insulin-dependent diabetes mellitus, preeclampsia, Huntington's chorea, and some rare genetic disorders. For example, in the case of genetic disorders like Fanconi's anemia and Bloom syndrome, the diseases progress because genes have been programmed to provide inadequate protection from free radicals. In another type of chronic disease, systemic lupus erythematosis (SLE), the immune system attacks connective tissue as if it were a toxic invader, causing inflammation. Some researchers suspect that an increased sensitivity to free-radical reactions, which can then be exacerbated by environmental factors such as a diet high in polyunsaturated fats, could contribute in part to the progressively destructive nature of a disease like SLE.

However, the extent of influence free-radical damage has on any of the above illnesses is not yet well documented. While you could make the logical assumption that an antioxidant-rich diet might be good preventive medicine, researchers feel it's too early in the game to even theorize about the impact of dietary antioxidants on these ailments. Stay informed as future research delves into these developing areas.

Meanwhile, you can still count on antioxidant-rich nutrients as potential weapons against more common ills like heart disease and cancer. And there is plenty of proof that these nutrient powerhouses are critical to a healthy immune system.

..............................

## Chapter 2

# Building an Antioxidant-Rich Diet

Now that you have a better understanding of the powerful health benefits of antioxidants, the next step is to figure out how to include more of these substances in your diet. In this chapter, we'll give you lists of foods rich in beta-carotene, selenium, vitamin E, and vitamin C; we'll even recap some of the research highlights. But the prime focus of this part of the book is to take you step by step through the process of building an antioxidant-rich diet. Since antioxidants are only one part of a healthful diet, make sure you understand and employ the latest recommendations for good nutrition. Promoted by the Department of Agriculture, this advice includes seven simple "dietary guidelines." It applies equally well to adults and children over the age of two.

- Eat a variety of foods.

- Maintain a healthy weight.

- Choose a diet low in fat, saturated fat, and cholesterol.

- Choose a diet with plenty of vegetables, fruits, and grain products.

- Use sugars only in moderation.

- Use salt and sodium only in moderation.

- If you drink alcoholic beverages, do so in moderation.

Once you've shaped up your overall diet, you'll be ready to focus on antioxidant-rich foods and dietary ingredients that may be able to inhibit free-radical reaction-induced damage. Since studies suggest that foods containing vitamin E, vitamin C, beta-carotene, or selenium seem capable of accomplishing this goal, your primary goal is to eat foods rich in these nutrients. That isn't hard to do when you dish up a colorful plate of Tuna Salad Composé, a main-dish salad from our recipe section that carries a triple dose of beta-carotene as well as healthy amounts of both selenium and vitamin C.

In fact, we have more than a hundred mouthwatering recipes to help you boost the antioxidant level of your diet simply by including more fruits, vegetables, and whole grains at each meal. There's everything from appetizers to soup to side dishes to salads to main courses. There are foods for breakfast—Strawberry-Mango Shake, Pumpkin-Nut Quick Bread—foods for snacking, and foods to satisfy the sweet tooth, all while boosting the antioxidant level of your diet.

At breakfast, instead of eating your dry cereal plain or with raisins, try Molasses-Nut Granola. It's a bit high in calories, but it's also nutrient dense. And not only does it offer healthy amounts of iron and fiber, but it contains small amounts of vitamin A and zinc as well. Or if you'd rather grab a muffin, try a family favorite, the Double-Apricot Oatmeal Muffins. Made with both pureed and dried apricots, this is a delicious way to incorporate more beta-carotene into your morning meal. When you factor in the 2 grams of fiber and only a few grams of fat, the overall nutrient profile seems unbeatable.

When you are eating out, make sure to carry on with an antioxidant-rich eating theme. Fall into the habit of weighing choices based on fruit and vegetable content. If you're eating at an Italian restaurant, instead of stuffed manicotti or fettuccine Alfredo—both of which contain a lot of cheese and fat—try a pasta with red sauce (tomatoes are rich in vitamin C) or a dish like pasta primavera, which is piled high with all kinds of colorful vegetables. Or better yet, stay at home and fix our iron- and selenium-rich Linguine with Clams, Red Peppers, and Broccoli.

As you'll begin to find, there's no limit on the amount of antioxidants you can build into your meals. Once you learn which fruits and which vegetables contain which nutrients, you'll find that the task of choosing powerhouse antioxidant foods becomes easier and easier.

## Beta-carotene

Technically not a nutrient, beta-carotene is one of a group of six hundred different carotenoids found in plants. Perhaps the most widely recognized of the antioxidants, this plant pigment lends a brilliant orange color to everything from pumpkin to carrots to cantaloupe. (Dark leafy greens like spinach and broccoli also contain beta-carotene, but chlorophyll masks the orange color.) And although it can be converted into vitamin A in the body, it's beta-carotene's ability to inactivate free radicals that makes it an outstanding contribution to any antiaging diet.

Research has identified a need for beta-carotene in keeping the immune system healthy. Numerous studies link diets rich in fruits and vegetables containing beta-carotene to a lower risk for a variety of cancers, including cancer of the lung and breast. And a wealth of compelling evidence supports a role for beta-carotene as a protector against both heart disease and cataracts.

*The recipes in this book have been analyzed for vitamin A, not beta-carotene.* Unfortunately, limited data is available on the exact beta-carotene content of foods. However, we'll note in the introduction to each recipe section the selections that are particularly high in beta-carotene. As a general rule of thumb, the bulk of vitamin A in fruits and vegetables comes from carotenoid compounds, predominantly beta-carotene.

## PROTECTIVE DOSE:

There is no Recommended Dietary Allowances (RDA) set for beta-carotene, but the National Cancer Institute has gone on record as recommending people eat about 5 to 6 milligrams per day, the amount found in 1/2 carrot, a very rich source, or 1 cup cooked broccoli plus 1 cup of cantaloupe. Early studies find that beta-carotene helps protect against cancer when intake is between 15 to 30 milligrams per day.

## TOXICITY PROBLEMS:

Most scientists believe that large quantities of beta-carotene are relatively safe. About the only problem some people experience is a yellow coloring to the skin, something that is easily remedied by cutting back on beta-carotene. Experts feel there's no way to overdose on beta-carotene rich foods.

## NUTRIENT CONSERVATION TIPS:

Nutrient levels in foods can vary widely depending on where they are grown. One analysis of carrots showed carotene levels that varied as much as twelvefold! But no matter what beta-carotene level you start with, there are steps you can take to make sure you preserve as much of this antioxidant as possible:

- Small amounts of beta-carotene can leach out from foods into cooking liquids. Use minimal amounts of water.

- Since any kind of processing can cause nutrient loss, you'll find the most beta-carotene in fresh produce rather than processed. One study found beta-carotene levels dropped 5 to 40 percent when foods were dried.

- Studies indicated that the outer, darker green leaves of cabbage and spinach are richest in beta-carotene, so try to salvage these leaves after washing thoroughly.

- Make sure to eat foods rich in beta-carotene at a meal that includes some fat. A breakfast of skim milk and no-fat cereal doesn't contain enough fat to help you absorb this fat-soluble antioxidant.

### Foods Containing Beta-carotene

Carrots receive top billing as prime sources of beta-carotene because they are a commonly eaten vegetable. But why not expand your horizons to include other beta-carotene–rich foods? When cantaloupe is in season, add a slice to breakfast. Or take time to make the luscious but low-fat Cantaloupe Granita found in the dessert section. With less than 0.5 gram of fat per serving, it definitely beats out ice cream. More importantly, it also contains nearly a full day's supply of beta-carotene and exceeds the recommended dose for vitamin C. Other rich sources of beta-carotene include main courses like Potato-Kale Frittata and Saffron Paella with Artichokes, Tomatoes, and Red Peppers as well as yummy desserts like Carrot Spice Cake and Sweet Potato Custard.

| FOOD ITEM | MILLIGRAMS OF BETA-CAROTENE |
|---|---|
| Sweet potato, ½ cup mashed | 16.8 mg |
| Pumpkin, ½ cup canned | 16.1 mg |
| Carrot, 1 medium, raw | 12.1 mg |
| Carrots, ½ cup cooked | 11.5 mg |
| Mango, 1 medium | 4.8 mg |
| Spinach, ½ cup boiled | 4.4 mg |
| Butternut squash, ½ cup cooked | 4.3 mg |
| Turnip greens, ½ cup boiled | 3.9 mg |
| Papaya, 1 medium | 3.7 mg |
| Cantaloupe, 1 cup | 3.1 mg |
| Collards, ½ cup boiled | 3.0 mg |

| Food Item | Milligrams of Beta-carotene |
|---|---|
| Kale, ½ cup boiled | 2.9 mg |
| Beet greens, ½ cup boiled | 2.2 mg |
| Winter squash, ½ cup baked | 2.2 mg |
| Persimmon, Japanese, 1 whole | 2.2 mg |
| Broccoli, 1 cup cooked | 2.1 mg |
| Mustard greens, ½ cup boiled | 2.0 mg |
| Apricots, 3 medium | 1.7 mg |
| Avocado, 1 medium | 1.1 mg |
| Parsley, ½ cup chopped | 0.9 mg |

*Source: Adapted from* Bowes and Church's Food Values of Portions Commonly Used, *16th ed. (Philadelphia: J. B. Lippincott Co., 1994).*

# Vitamin C

Vital to helping the body fight infections, including the common cold, vitamin C is receiving attention for some very important other reasons. Studies show that this nutrient, along with other antioxidants, may help delay the onset of cataracts. It's also been cited as a potential cancer fighter and a protector against heart disease.

*The recipes in this book have been analyzed for vitamin C.*

### PROTECTIVE DOSE:

While the recommended dietary allowance (RDA) is set at 60 milligrams, the dose of vitamin C needed to help stave off heart disease, cataracts, cancer, and other ills appears to be somewhat higher. Scientists won't be pinned down to exact numbers, but current estimates favor a defensive prescription that's somewhere in the range of 100 to 500 milligrams per day. Recipes like the Basil–Red Pepper Soup (239 milligrams of vitamin C), a favorite selection from the soup category, and the spectacularly colored Layered Roasted Vegetable Terrine (212 milligrams) are particularly rich and tasty sources.

### TOXICITY PROBLEMS:

Although excess amounts of vitamin C are typically excreted, megadoses of this nutrient have, in rare instances, created problems such as kidney stones in certain susceptible people.

Relying on single-dose supplements as your vitamin C source is not only a culinary bore, but it's also more likely to present overdose problems. On the other hand, it's unlikely you will experience any harmful side effects from vitamin C–rich foods. A "comfort food" like the Turnip-Potato Puree and an elegant indulgence like the Strawberry Soup with Balsamic Vinegar deliver vitamin C in laudable but tasty amounts.

## NUTRIENT CONSERVATION TIPS:

The most fragile of the antioxidants and one of the two most fragile vitamins (along with thiamine), vitamin C is very sensitive to destruction. Exposure to air (oxygen), light, heat, water, and the passage of time all conspire to destroy this vulnerable nutrient. Careful attention to storage, processing, and cooking can keep you one step ahead of any big nutrient losses.

- Eat the edible skin or peel on fruits, potatoes, and other produce whenever possible. The highest concentration of vitamin C is found in the layer just beneath a potato's skin. Ditto for most other produce.

- Emphasize nutrient-dense parts of vegetables. The outer leaves of spinach and cabbage, if you can salvage them, have the highest concentration of vitamin C. Broccoli florets have more vitamin C than stalks.

- Chill fruits and vegetables. Try to purchase produce that is ripe and ready to eat so you won't need to ripen outside the refrigerator. Produce left at room temperature for one day has been shown to lose as much as 30 to 40 percent of its vitamin C content. One caveat: Storing tomatoes in the refrigerator alters texture and sometimes taste, so it's a trade-off on texture and taste versus vitamin C content.

- Store produce in airtight packages or in the produce bin of your refrigerator because loss of moisture accelerates vitamin C loss.

- Cut or chop produce just before serving. The more surface area you expose of a fruit or vegetable, the higher the vitamin C loss. Sliced cantaloupe stored in a refrigerator for 24 hours has been shown to lose 35 percent of its vitamin C.

- Use as little water as possible for cooking, since vitamin C is water soluble and can leach out into cooking liquid. Vegetables lose almost half their vitamin C content when bathed in water to cover during cooking. Using only ½ cup of water in the pot cuts vitamin C losses 10 percent, and steaming vegetables can result in even smaller losses.

- Cook vegetables quickly, since heat destroys vitamin C. Pressure cooking (superheated steam in an airtight container) helps preserve vitamin C better than boiling or regular steaming. Microwaving, since it is quick and calls for little water, is also good.

### Foods Containing Vitamin C

Don't limit yourself to orange juice at breakfast or other citrus fruits as your sole source of vitamin C. Venture into the realm of tropical fruits—kiwi, papaya, mango, cantaloupe—with the tart but sweet Tropical Fruit Salad found in the dessert section. It packs a powerful vitamin C punch and makes a fun, colorful start or finish to any meal. Or try the easy-to-fix, main-course Pasta, Broccoli, and Basil Salad. Broccoli furnishes a hefty dose of vitamin C, but it's the feta cheese, onions, and red wine dressing that elevates this Greek-flavored main dish to something special.

| FOOD | MILLIGRAMS OF VITAMIN C |
|---|---|
| Papaya, 1 medium | 188 mg |
| Yellow pepper, 1/2 medium | 170 mg |
| Guava, 1 medium | 165 mg |
| Orange juice, 8 oz. | 124 mg |
| Broccoli, 1 cup cooked | 98 mg |
| Red pepper, 1/2 cup chopped | 95 mg |
| Strawberries, 1 cup | 85 mg |
| Kiwi fruit, 1 medium | 75 mg |
| Grapefruit juice, 8 oz. | 72 mg |
| Cantaloupe, 1 cup | 68 mg |
| Mango, 1 medium | 57 mg |
| Tomato paste, 1/2 cup | 55 mg |
| Cherimoya, 1 medium | 49 mg |
| Brussel sprouts, 1/2 cup cooked (4) | 48 mg |
| Kohlrabi, 1/2 cup boiled | 44 mg |
| Mandarin orange, 1/2 cup | 43 mg |

| | |
|---|---|
| Gooseberries, 1 cup | 42 mg |
| Honeydew melon, 1 cup | 42 mg |
| Cauliflower, 1/2 cup cooked | 36 mg |
| Raspberries, 1 cup | 31 mg |
| Asparagus, 8 spears cooked | 30 mg |
| Blackberries, 1 cup | 30 mg |
| Sweet potato, 1 | 28 mg |
| Carambola, 1 medium | 27 mg |
| Amaranth, 1/2 cup boiled | 27 mg |
| Kale, 1/2 cup boiled | 27 mg |
| Pineapple juice, 8 oz. | 27 mg |
| Tomato, 1 medium | 24 mg |
| Snow peas, 3 oz. | 24 mg |
| Pineapple, 1 cup raw | 24 mg |
| Collards, 1/2 cup boiled | 23 mg |
| Chinese cabbage, 1/2 cup boiled | 22 mg |
| Parsley, 1/4 cup chopped | 20 mg |
| Blueberries, 1 cup | 19 mg |
| Mustard greens, 1/2 cup boiled | 18 mg |
| Cabbage, 1/2 cup shredded raw | 17 mg |
| Beet greens, 1/2 cup boiled | 18 mg |
| Persimmon, 1 medium | 17 mg |
| Spinach, 1 cup raw | 16 mg |

| FOOD | MILLIGRAMS OF VITAMIN C |
|------|-------------------------|
| *Radishes, ¹/₂ cup sliced* | *15 mg* |
| *Avocado, 1 medium* | *14 mg* |
| *Cranberries, 1 cup* | *13 mg* |
| *Artichoke, 1 medium* | *12 mg* |

*Source: Adapted from Bowes and Church's Food Values of Portions Commonly Used, 16th ed. (Philadelphia: J. B. Lippincott Co., 1994).*

## Vitamin E

Vitamin E ranks as possibly the most potent of the antioxidant nutrients. It's wide-reaching protective benefits impact everything from immune health to heart disease to cataracts and other eye ailments. To recap: Studies show that vitamin E may help shield against cataracts and macular degeneration, two eye disorders of old age. Vitamin E appears to improve certain aspects of immune responsiveness that weaken with age. And two major research reports link diets rich in vitamin E (subjects in the study used supplements) with lower risk of heart disease in both men and women.

*We could not analyze the recipes in this book for vitamin E content as there is only limited data available.* However, we'll note in the introductions of each recipe category the recipes that contain small amounts of this key antioxidant.

**PROTECTIVE DOSE:**

Research points out that the dose of this antioxidant needed to protect against illness is far higher than the current RDA, which is set at 10 milligrams of alpha tocopherol equivalents for men and 8 milligrams for women. Short-term studies hint that amounts as high as 100 to 400 milligrams of vitamin E per day may be both safe and beneficial. However, research is currently underway to determine if smaller amounts of vitamin E for over a longer time period might be just as effective.

**TOXICITY PROBLEMS:**

Despite the fact that it's a fat-soluble vitamin (so any excess you take in is stored in fat tissues), scientists have found little evidence of toxicity for vitamin E.

**NUTRIENT CONSERVATION TIPS:**

Little research has been done on how cooking affects the vitamin E content of foods. As it is a fat-soluble vitamin, and because it is less fragile than nutrients like vitamin C, you can probably count on the vitamin E content of food changing very little during cooking.

### Foods Containing Vitamin E

Because a large concentration of vitamin E is found in high-fat items like vegetable oils and products made from these oils such as margarine, it isn't easy to boost your vitamin E intake while keeping your diet low in fat. In fact, many researchers are convinced that most people are unlikely to be able to tap into the potential benefits of vitamin E through foods alone and so recommend vitamin E supplements. It's not impossible to boost your intake of vitamin E. But the fact remains that even the recipes in this book are only able to add small amounts of vitamin E to your diet.

For example, leafy greens and sweet potatoes contain modest amounts of the vitamin, making salads and main dishes like the Shepherd's Pie with Sweet Potato Topping a good start. You can also do a lot to boost your vitamin E intake by simply sprinkling a few tablespoons of wheat germ onto your morning cereal. Each 2 tablespoons contains slightly more than 2 milligrams of vitamin E (expressed as equivalents of the alpha tocopherol form of this nutrient) or 20 percent of the recommended daily allowance.

| FOOD ITEM | MILLIGRAMS OF VITAMIN E (EXPRESSED AS ALPHA TOCOPHEROL) |
|---|---|
| Sunflower seeds, 1 oz. | 14.2 mg |
| Hazelnuts, 1 oz. | 6.7 mg |
| Almonds, 1 oz. (24 nuts) | 6.7 mg |
| Sweet potato, cooked, 1 medium | 5.9 mg |
| Cottonseed oil, 1 tablespoon | 4.8 mg |
| Safflower oil, 1 tablespoon | 4.6 mg |
| Wheat germ, ¼ cup (1 oz.) | 4.1 mg |
| Peanut butter, 2 tablespoons | 3.0 mg |
| Peanuts, 1 oz. roasted | 2.6 mg |
| Avocado, 1 medium | 2.3 mg |
| Mango, 1 medium | 2.3 mg |
| Corn oil, 1 tablespoon | 1.9 mg |

| FOOD ITEM | MILLIGRAMS OF VITAMIN E |
|---|---|
| | (EXPRESSED AS ALPHA TOCOPHEROL) |
| Spinach, raw, 1 cup chopped | 1.0 mg |
| Apricots, 4 halves canned | 0.8 mg |
| Asparagus, ½ cup | 0.8 mg |
| Walnuts, 1 oz. | 0.7 mg |
| Turnip greens, ½ cup raw | 0.6 mg |
| Mustard greens, ½ cup raw | 0.6 mg |

Source: Adapted from Bowes and Church's Food Values of Portions Commonly Used, 16th ed. (Philadelphia: J. B. Lippincott Co., 1994).

### Do You Need Vitamin E Supplements?

Experts at the Food and Nutrition Board of the National Academy of Sciences, the scientists who set the RDAs (Recommended Dietary Allowances) for nutrients, contend there is little evidence to support the benefits of vitamin E supplements. Yet preliminary new evidence hints that supplements may help to boost immune function and protect against heart disease, at least in certain people. Even if it's too soon to make any general recommendations, some researchers point out that in doses of 100 to 400 mg a day, supplemental vitamin E is relatively nontoxic. One caveat: Be aware that the synthetic form of vitamin E is not quite as potent as the form found naturally in foods.

## Selenium

A trace mineral (one of those substances that is present in the body in minuscule amounts yet is critically important to health), selenium often works in tandem with vitamin E. The two antioxidants together make a powerful team, yet preliminary reports find that selenium may act alone to block tumors and the spread of cancer. In laboratory studies, researchers find that selenium is needed to keep certain components of the immune system healthy, namely the natural killer (NK) cells that can destroy tumors and the T-lymphocytes, white blood cells that help the immune system recognize and mount a defense against foreign toxins.

We couldn't analyze these recipes for selenium. That's primarily because there is not a lot of detailed data regarding the selenium content of foods. However, we'll note in the introduction which recipes contain selenium.

### PROTECTIVE DOSE:

The Recommended Dietary Allowance for selenium is 70 micrograms. Some experts feel that the protective dose probably exceeds that amount, but research is very preliminary.

### TOXICITY PROBLEMS:

Helpful as this antioxidant appears to be, it is possible to overdose if you try obtaining your selenium through supplements. People taking 5 milligrams of selenium per day have experienced hair loss and loss of fingernails. More importantly, an excess of the nutrient can hinder immune response.

### NUTRIENT CONSERVATION TIPS:

Minerals are far less fragile than vitamins and so are not damaged as easily by heat, processing or exposure to air. In fact, studies document that there is very little difference in the mineral content of raw, frozen, or canned foods.

### FOOD SOURCES:

Seafoods are rich in selenium. So when you serve up a personal favorite—whether the Swordfish with Mango Salsa or the Linguine with Clams, Red Peppers, and Broccoli—you'll be dishing up a generous helping of this trace mineral. In hot weather, try selenium-rich seafood in a main dish like the Tuna Salad Composé or the Italian Seafood Salad. Made with shrimp, scallops, mussels, and green olives, this is a rich and delicious summer meal. Be aware that whole grains do contain small amounts of selenium, so bakery items like the Raspberry-Walnut Muffins make a tiny but helpful contribution to your daily selenium totals.

## Zinc

While zinc is not an antioxidant nutrient, its profound effect on the immune system makes it critical to any diet aimed at trying to slow down the aging process while maximizing health and immune response. A deficiency of zinc can interfere with the normal development of white blood cells and fast-acting immune cells that annihilate toxins and foreign substances. *The recipes in this book have been analyzed for zinc content.*

### PROTECTIVE DOSE:

The RDA and the protective dose for zinc—15 milligrams—seem to be one and the same.

### TOXICITY PROBLEMS:

Zinc is a relatively nontoxic nutrient. But that doesn't totally rule out a potential for toxicity when someone megadoses on zinc supplements. Overdosing via supplements can lead to vomiting, diarrhea, and possibly more serious problems.

## NUTRIENT CONSERVATION TIPS:

As mentioned before, minerals are far less fragile than vitamins and so tend to be relatively stable when exposed to light, air, heat, and prolonged storage times. Yet, there are a few strategies you may want to keep in mind.

- Cook zinc-rich vegetables in a minimal amount of water since, surprisingly, minerals do leach out into cooking liquids. Scientists noticed a 25 percent drop in another important mineral—calcium—when vegetables were cooked in water to cover. Less of the mineral was lost when water levels were decreased.

- Eat the skin of produce. When you peel fruits and vegetables, you lose some of the zinc.

- Choose whole grains over refined grain products. When manufacturers remove the outer bran coating of grains, zinc and other important nutrients are lost.

### *Foods That Contain Zinc*

Zinc is easily obtained from almost all protein-containing foods. That list includes everything from lean meats and seafood to vegetables to whole grains. However, you will notice that the selections in the Meat, Fish, and Poultry/Main Dish section are the only ones that are truly rich in zinc, since the mineral concentrates in animal meats. Nevertheless, if you eat a wide variety of foods and keep your fruit, vegetable, and grain intake high, you'll have no difficulty meeting zinc requirements.

| FOOD ITEM | MILLIGRAMS OF ZINC |
|---|---|
| Oysters, 3 oz. cooked (12 medium) | 154.6 mg |
| Ground beef, extra lean, 3½ oz. cooked | 6.9 mg |
| Sirloin steak, 3½ oz. cooked | 6.5 mg |
| Veal, ground, 3½ oz. cooked | 3.9 mg |
| Clams, 3 oz. cooked | 2.3 mg |
| Chicken, dark, 3½ oz. roasted | 2.8 mg |
| Chickpeas (garbanzo beans), 1 cup cooked | 2.5 mg |

| FOOD ITEM | MILLIGRAMS OF ZINC |
|---|---|
| Lentils, 1 cup cooked | 2.5 mg |
| Split peas, 1 cup boiled | 2.0 mg |
| Black beans, 1 cup cooked | 1.9 mg |
| Kidney beans, 1 cup cooked | 1.9 mg |
| Pinto beans, 1 cup cooked | 1.9 mg |
| Lima beans, 1 cup cooked | 1.8 mg |
| Hominy, 1 cup cooked | 1.7 mg |
| Black-eyed peas, 1 cup cooked | 1.7 mg |
| Spinach, 1 cup cooked | 1.4 mg |
| Chicken, white, 3½ oz. roasted | 1.2 mg |
| Shrimp, 3 oz. cooked | 1.3 mg |
| Swordfish, 3 oz. cooked | 1.3 mg |
| Squid, 3 oz. raw | 1.3 mg |
| Rainbow trout, 3 oz. cooked | 1.2 mg |
| Canned tuna, 3 oz. drained | 0.8 mg |
| Yellowfin Tuna, 3 oz. cooked | 0.6 mg |
| Salmon, pink, 3 oz. cooked | 0.6 mg |

Source: Bowes and Church's Food Values of Portions Commonly Used, 16th ed.
(Philadelphia: J. B. Lippincott Co., 1994).

## Other Protective Agents

While the bulk of attention seems focused on nutrients and their potential antiaging abilities, researchers do point out other dietary ingredients that may have an impact on aging. For instance, scientists have long known that cruciferous vegetables—cabbage, broccoli, brussels sprouts, and other members of the mustard family—seem capable of protecting against cancer. Initially, researchers identified the protective agents as indoles. However, scientists from

Johns Hopkins Medical Institute in Baltimore find that sulforophane, a chemical found in high concentrations in broccoli, has potent cancer-fighting ability. Laboratory studies show that sulforophane can boost the production of enzymes that fight cancer. And studies have already confirmed that the chemical is capable of fighting cancer in animals.

Also important may be plant compounds called flavonoids (quercetin, kaempherol, myricetin, apigenin, and luteolin), natural antioxidants that are present in many fruits and vegetables as well as beverages like tea and wine. Lab studies find that flavonoids can inhibit the oxidation of LDL, the heart-harmful or "bad" cholesterol package. A recent English study looked at flavonoid intake and the risk of heart disease death among a large group of older men. After adjusting for other variables—smoking, vitamin C, vitamin E, beta-carotene, fiber, total calories, etc.—researchers noticed that men who regularly ate flavonoid-rich foods were at significantly less risk of death from cardiovascular disease than those who ate very little. Tea, onions, and apples were the richest flavonoid sources in the men's diets.

Rather than boost your intake of apples and onions, however, experts recommend broadening your diet focus to include more fruits and vegetables, period. Keep in mind that it may take years or it may never be possible to identify each and every compound in fruits and vegetables that confers healthful benefits. Then again, it's not really necessary. All you need to do to ensure an optimum and healthy lifespan is to build fruits and vegetables into a prudent low-fat diet. Round out that plant-rich plan with whole grains, seafood, and lean meats and you'll receive the full complement of nature's potent diet medicine.

To help you get started on this antioxidant-phytochemical–rich eating plan, we've developed a week's worth of menus incorporating a myriad of antioxidant-rich foods fixed in a variety of delicious ways.

Chapter 3

# Seven-Day Antioxidant-Rich Menu Plan

Using the recipes in this cookbook—which are moderately low in fat, cholesterol, and sodium—can help you to emphasize fruits and vegetables that are particularly good sources of the antioxidant nutrients beta-carotene, vitamin C, selenium, and vitamin E. Our seven-day menu plan offers an assortment of mouthwatering meals. You can choose to follow the menu plan precisely, or simply use it as a model for developing your own antioxidant-rich diet. Nosh on antioxidant-rich but tasty appetizers like Spinach-Jalapeño Quesadillas, Tomato Crostini, or Whole-Wheat Garlic Chips. Or dazzle and satisfy friends and family with incredible-tasting main courses like the Thai-inspired Mango and Fennel Salad with Shrimp and Peanuts, a rich source of beta-carotene with notable amounts of iron, zinc, and vitamin C.

In general, we've followed the guidelines for healthy eating presented in the Food Guide Pyramid below.

# The Food Guide Pyramid
## A Guide to Daily Food Choices

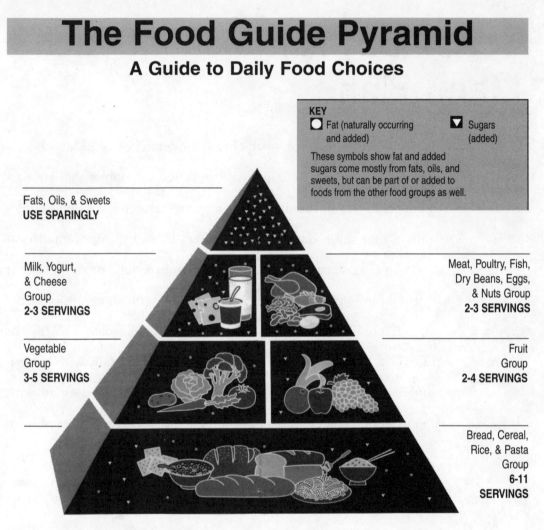

**KEY**
◯ Fat (naturally occurring and added)   ▼ Sugars (added)

These symbols show fat and added sugars come mostly from fats, oils, and sweets, but can be part of or added to foods from the other food groups as well.

Fats, Oils, & Sweets
**USE SPARINGLY**

Milk, Yogurt,
& Cheese
Group
**2-3 SERVINGS**

Meat, Poultry, Fish,
Dry Beans, Eggs,
& Nuts Group
**2-3 SERVINGS**

Vegetable
Group
**3-5 SERVINGS**

Fruit
Group
**2-4 SERVINGS**

Bread, Cereal,
Rice, & Pasta
Group
**6-11
SERVINGS**

To order a copy of "The Food Guide Pyramid" booklet, send a $1.00 check or money order made out to the Superintendent of Documents to: Consumer Information Center, Department 159-Y, Pueblo, Colorado 81009.

U.S. Department of Agriculture, Human Nutrition Information Service, August 1992, Leaflet No. 572

We've made sure that fat provides no more than 30 percent of the total calories each day and that saturated fat accounts for no more than one third of that total. Daily sodium levels fall within the recommended guidelines (2,400 milligrams per day) and cholesterol levels stay well under the 300-milligram daily limit set by the American Heart Association. But if you have any special health concerns, make sure to review the nutrient profile that accompanies the recipe. It can help you to put recipes into the context of your total dietary needs.

You will notice that each recipe in this book has been analyzed for calories, total fat, saturated fat, sodium, fiber, and cholesterol. Also, information is included about the iron, zinc, vitamin A, and vitamin C content of individual foods. If you need to increase the amount of iron in your diet, you'll be happy to hear that the recipes we've developed contain plentiful amounts of iron. Many are also rich in calcium. In other words, these recipes are not only rich in antioxidants but they will boost the overall quality of your diet. Note: Menu items made from recipes in this book are noted with an *.

## MONDAY

### Breakfast
Tropical Fruit Salad* with mango
Oatmeal Buttermilk Pancakes* with
maple syrup and margarine
Orange juice
Low-fat (1%) milk
Coffee or tea

### Lunch
Pasta, Broccoli, and Basil Salad*
Whole-wheat roll with margarine
Raspberry-Orange Frozen Yogurt*
Iced tea with lemon

### Supper
Fish Cooked in Spicy Tomato Sauce*
Baked Sweet Potato Fries*
Steamed kale
Almond Angel Food Cake with
Mango Puree*
Coffee or tea

### Snack
Whole-Wheat Garlic Chips*
Cranberry juice spritzer

## TUESDAY

### Breakfast
Molasses-Nut Granola*
Low-fat (1%) milk
Double-Apricot Oatmeal Muffin*
Grapefruit juice
Coffee or tea

### Lunch
Sliced Steak and Roasted Tomato Salad*
French bread with margarine
Sliced strawberries with kiwifruit
Coffee or tea

### Supper
Shepherd's Pie with Sweet
Potato Topping*
Summer Tomato Salad*

*continued*

Cantaloupe Granita*
Coffee or tea

*Snack*
Tropical Citrus Shake*

## WEDNESDAY

*Breakfast*
Fresh sliced cantaloupe
Pumpkin-Nut Quick Bread*
Low-fat yogurt
Coffee or tea

*Lunch*
Carrot-Papaya Coleslaw*
Lean roast beef sandwich on whole-grain
bread with sliced tomatoes
Apricot Square*
Iced tea with lemon

*Supper*
Braised Chicken with Apricots and Ginger*
Turnip-Potato Puree*
Steamed carrots
Pumpkin Pie*
Coffee or tea

*Snack*
Raspberry-Orange Frozen Yogurt*

## THURSDAY

*Breakfast*
Whole-grain cereal flakes
2 tablespoons wheat germ
Raspberry-Walnut Muffin

Low-fat (1%) milk
Grapefruit juice
Coffee or tea

*Lunch*
Tuna Salad Composé*
Whole-grain roll with margarine
Spice-poached Fruit Compote*
Coffee or iced tea

*Supper*
Oven-steamed Salmon with Roast Pepper
and Onion Compote*
Wild Rice with Oranges and Scallions*
Steamed broccoli
Sweet Potato Custard*
Coffee or tea

*Snack*
Spritzer made with orange juice
Raspberry-Walnut Muffin*

## FRIDAY

*Breakfast*
Double-Apricot Oatmeal Muffin*
Bitter Orange and Apricot Marmalade*
Oatmeal with brown sugar and
1 tablespoon slivered almonds
Low-fat (1%) milk
Coffee or tea

*Lunch*
Brown Rice with Vegetables and Almonds*
Watercress Salad with Oranges and
Grapefruit*
Tomato juice

*Supper*
Citrus–Pinto Bean Dip*
No-fat tortilla chips
Carrot and celery sticks
Southwestern Chicken and Rice Salad*
Tropical Fruit Salad*

*Snack*
Sliced mango with kiwifruit

## SATURDAY

*Breakfast*
Hot Wheatberry Cereal*
Raspberry-Walnut Muffin*
Orange juice
Coffee or tea

*Lunch*
Carrot and Broccoli Risotto*
Whole-grain bread
Iced tea with lemon

*Supper*
Tomato Crostini*
Spinach Salad with Fresh Raspberry
Vinaigrette*
Linguine with Clams, Red Peppers, and
Broccoli*
Red wine spritzer
Fresh orange slices
Coffee or tea

*Snack*
Apricot Square*
Low-fat (1%) milk

## SUNDAY

*Breakfast*
Tropical Fruit Salad*
Potato-Kale Frittata*
Fruit juice cocktail (made with orange
juice, cranberry juice, and lime)
Whole-wheat toast
Bitter Orange and Apricot Marmalade*

*Lunch*
Parsley–White Bean Dip*
Carrot and celery sticks
Chicken–Wild Rice Salad with Mango and
Ginger*
Iced tea with lemon

*Supper*
Fennel and Orange Salad with Parsley and
Olives*
Tomato-stuffed Pork Tenderloin with
Roasted Poblano Sauce*
Roasted Butternut Squash and Garlic
Puree*
Steamed fresh spinach
Coffee or tea

*Snack*
Macerated Persimmons with Lemon*

| | |
|---|---|
| gm | grams |
| mg | milligrams |
| IU | International Units |
| < | less than |
| tr | trace |
| % | percent |

*The nutrition analyses in this book were provided by Hill Nutrition Associates. When a choice of ingredients is provided, please note that the nutrition analysis is based on the first possibility. Also, when an ingredient is marked "optional," it is not included in the recipe analysis.*

## Chapter 4

# Appetizers and Snacks

Now that nibbling is practically a national pastime, why not have some recipes on hand that can dish up a healthy amount of antioxidant protection? The dips, snacks, and party fare that follow are all tasty morsels guaranteed to cause raves among your guests. None of the selections are difficult to whip up, and the choices are versatile enough to fit into just about any kind of party or snacking theme. In the mood for Mexican? Try the navy bean dip that's spiked with citrus and jalapeños or the Avocado and Tomato Salsa. Both deliver south of the border flavor along with a healthy punch of vitamin C.

Or why not pair appetizers like Sweet and Hot Pepper Crostini (you can mix and match different varieties of peppers) and one of my favorites, marinated vegetables, for a taste of the Mediterranean. Both appetizers provide nearly triple the recommended dose of vitamin C, plus a generous allotment of beta-carotene. Sit down with a bowl of crunchy Whole-Wheat Garlic Chips the next time you plug a movie into the VCR and boost your fiber and iron intake. Indeed, with nearly a dozen different munching options, you can satisfy your munchies while netting health benefits as well.

# Spinach-Jalapeño Quesadillas

• This is an easy appetizer or snack that can be put together in a pinch. Try experimenting with different fillings, or add cooked chicken and serve as a main course.

Preparation time: 10 minutes

Cooking time: 5 minutes

Serves 4

| | |
|---|---|
| 1 jalapeño pepper, seeded and minced | 1 medium tomato, thinly sliced (1 cup) |
| 2 cups chopped fresh spinach | 2 cloves garlic, minced |
| 4 10-inch flour tortillas | ½ teaspoon freshly ground black pepper |
| 1½ ounces shredded Monterey jack or cheddar cheese | |

**1.** Heat large nonstick skillet over medium heat. Add jalapeño and cook 2 minutes, stirring occasionally, until soft. Add spinach; cook until just wilted; remove mixture from pan. Wipe out pan.

**2.** Place one tortilla in pan; sprinkle one half of the tortilla with one quarter of the cheese, then top the cheese with one quarter of the spinach mixture, then of the tomato slices. Sprinkle with garlic and pepper.

**3.** Fold tortilla in half, pressing down until even. Heat 2 minutes, until bottom is golden, pressing down with spatula. Turn; continue cooking 2 minutes, until second side is golden and cheese is melted.

**4.** Repeat with remaining tortillas and filling. Cut in triangles to serve.

*continued*

## Nutrients Per Serving

| | | | | | |
|---|---|---|---|---|---|
| Calories: | 238 | Cholesterol: | 11 mg | Vitamin A: | 2991 IU |
| Fat: | 7.3 gm | Sodium: | 347 mg | Vitamin C: | 26 mg |
| Sat. fat: | 2.5 gm | Fiber: | 3.1 gm | Zinc: | .9 mg |
| Iron: | 2.9 mg | Cal. from fat: | 28% | | |

# Ginger-marinated Tuna Salad

- This delicately flavored fish salad is a lovely way to begin a meal. The fish "cooks" in the marinade, and the Asian flavors will transport you to Japan.

Preparation time: 10 minutes

Marinating time: 40 minutes

Serves 4

1 tablespoon reduced-sodium soy sauce

3 tablespoons fresh lemon juice

2 tablespoons safflower oil

1 tablespoon grated fresh ginger

1 pound best-quality fresh tuna, about 1 inch thick

¼ cup thinly sliced scallions

**1.** In large bowl, combine soy sauce, lemon juice, safflower oil, and ginger. Stir well.

**2.** Add tuna. Cover and refrigerate 40 minutes, turning fish after 20 minutes.

**3.** Slice fish very thin. Arrange on serving plates. Drizzle remaining marinade on top. Sprinkle with scallions.

### Nutrients Per Serving

| Calories: | 201 | Cholesterol: | 43 mg | Vitamin A: | 2,505 IU |
|---|---|---|---|---|---|
| Fat: | 9 gm | Sodium: | 198 mg | Vitamin C: | 4 mg |
| Sat. fat: | 1.7 gm | Fiber: | tr | Zinc: | .7 mg |
| Iron: | 1.3 mg | Cal. from fat: | 40% | | |

# Parsley–White Bean Dip

• This herb-packed dip is ideal for company. Just whir it up in the food processor and share the health. It is creamy and smooth without the sour cream or mayonnaise of most dips.

Serve with fresh vegetable crudités.

Preparation time: 5 minutes

Cooking time: None

Serves 4

3 cups cooked cannellini or other white beans (or canned, drained and rinsed)

1 cup (packed) Italian (flat-leaf) parsley leaves

¼ cup fresh lemon juice

1 tablespoon fresh rosemary leaves, blanched quickly in boiling water

1 tablespoon extra virgin olive oil

1 clove garlic, minced

½ teaspoon grated lemon zest

½ teaspoon freshly ground black pepper

Salt, to taste (optional)

Water, as needed

1. In food processor, combine beans, parsley, lemon juice, rosemary, olive oil, garlic, zest, pepper, and salt in the bowl of a food processor. Process until smooth, adding water 1 tablespoon at a time as necessary.

### Nutrients Per Serving

| Calories: | 154 | Cholesterol: | 0 | Vitamin A: | 669 IU |
|-----------|-----|--------------|---|-----------|--------|
| Fat: | 2.7 gm | Sodium: | 13 mg | Vitamin C: | 14.5 mg |
| Sat. fat: | .4 gm | Fiber: | 4.8 gm | Zinc: | 1.3 mg |
| Iron: | 4.3 mg | Cal. from fat: | 16% | | |

# Citrus–Pinto Bean Dip

- This tangy spicy bean dip is great for parties. Your guests will love it, and they won't know it's so good for them. Serve with fresh vegetable crudités, or try it with no-fat tortilla chips.

Preparation time: 5 minutes

Cooking time: 1 minute

Serves 4

½ teaspoon ground cumin

½ teaspoon cayenne pepper

2 cups cooked pinto beans (or canned, drained and rinsed)

½ cup (loosely packed) fresh cilantro leaves

½ cup tomato paste

¼ cup orange juice, fresh or from concentrate

¼ cup fresh lime juice

1 tablespoon grated orange zest

2 teaspoons safflower oil

1 jalapeño pepper, seeded and minced

1 large clove garlic, minced

Freshly ground black pepper, to taste

Salt, to taste (optional)

1 cup finely diced red bell pepper

1. In small skillet, heat the cumin and cayenne, over very low heat, just until fragrant, about 1 minute.

2. In food processor, combine cumin and cayenne with beans, cilantro, tomato paste, juices, zest, oil, jalapeño, garlic, pepper, and salt. Process until smooth.

3. Stir in red pepper.

### Nutrients Per Serving

| | | | | | | |
|---|---|---|---|---|---|---|
| Calories: | 201 | Cholesterol: | 0 | Vitamin A: | 2,435 IU |
| Fat: | 3.2 gm | Sodium: | 264 mg | Vitamin C: | 81 mg |
| Sat. fat: | .4 gm | Fiber: | 5.1 gm | Zinc: | 1.3 mg |
| Iron: | 3.6 mg | Cal. from fat: | 14% | | |

# Provençal Tuna Spread

• This tasty spread will take you to the south of France. Serve on toast squares as an hors d'oeuvre, at lunchtime in a sandwich with tomato and greens, or as a dip with fresh vegetable crudités.

Preparation time: 10 minutes

Cooking time: None

Serves 6

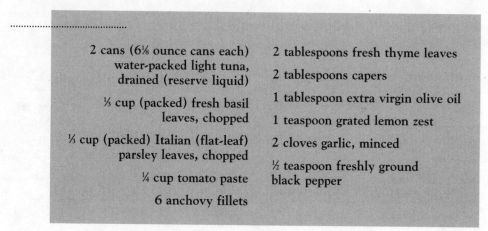

2 cans (6⅛ ounce cans each) water-packed light tuna, drained (reserve liquid)

⅓ cup (packed) fresh basil leaves, chopped

⅓ cup (packed) Italian (flat-leaf) parsley leaves, chopped

¼ cup tomato paste

6 anchovy fillets

2 tablespoons fresh thyme leaves

2 tablespoons capers

1 tablespoon extra virgin olive oil

1 teaspoon grated lemon zest

2 cloves garlic, minced

½ teaspoon freshly ground black pepper

1. In bowl of food processor, combine tuna, basil, parsley, tomato paste, anchovies, thyme, capers, oil, zest, garlic, and pepper. Puree until chunky, not smooth.

2. Stir in reserved tuna liquid to taste, until texture is creamy.

### Nutrients Per Serving

| Calories: | 108 | Cholesterol: | 23 mg | Vitamin A: | 691.38 IU |
|---|---|---|---|---|---|
| Fat: | 3.3 gm | Sodium: | 559 mg | Vitamin C: | 11 mg |
| Sat. fat: | .5 gm | Fiber: | .7 gm | Zinc: | .7 mg |
| Iron: | 3 mg | Cal. from fat: | 27% | | |

# Spinach Spread

• This easy spread is packed with iron and vitamin A. It is great as an hors d'oeuvre, or try as a sandwich filling, with tomatoes, for a healthy quick meal or snack.

Preparation time: 8 minutes, plus 4 hours refrigeration

Cooking time: 10 minutes

Serves 4

| | |
|---|---|
| 1 teaspoon safflower oil | 3 tablespoons fresh lemon juice |
| 1 cup chopped onion | 3 tablespoons grated parmesan cheese |
| 2 cloves garlic, minced | ½ teaspoon grated lemon zest |
| 2 packages (10 ounces each) frozen chopped spinach, thawed | ½ teaspoon freshly ground black pepper |
| ½ cup water | ⅛ teaspoon grated nutmeg |
| 1 cup low-fat cottage cheese | Salt, to taste (optional) |

**1.** In large nonstick skillet, heat oil over medium heat. Cook onion and garlic until onion is tender, 6 to 7 minutes.

**2.** Add spinach and water and cook until warm.

**3.** Transfer mixture to food processor, along with cottage cheese, juice, parmesan, zest, pepper, nutmeg, and salt (if used). Puree until smooth. Refrigerate 4 hours before serving to allow flavors to blend.

## Nutrients Per Serving

| | | | | | |
|---|---|---|---|---|---|
| Calories: | 123 | Cholesterol: | 5 mg | Vitamin A: | 11,047 IU |
| Fat: | 3.4 gm | Sodium: | 408 mg | Vitamin C: | 41 mg |
| Sat. fat: | 1.3 gm | Fiber: | 3.7 gm | Zinc: | 1 mg |
| Iron: | 3 mg | Cal. from fat: | 25% | | |

# Whole-Wheat Garlic Chips

- Who ever thought of making homemade crackers? These crisp and hearty crackers are a healthy, low-fat alternative to chips. They are fabulous served with any light dip and a great way to take in a little extra vitamin E. Try them with the Spinach Spread (page 51) for a great snack.

Preparation time: 10 minutes

Cooking time: 10 minutes

Makes about 50 crackers

| | |
|---|---|
| ½ cup whole-wheat flour | ½ teaspoon freshly ground black pepper |
| ½ cup all-purpose flour | ½ teaspoon salt |
| ¼ cup wheat germ | ¼ cup plain low-fat yogurt |
| 3 cloves garlic, minced | 1 tablespoon safflower oil |
| 2 teaspoons sugar | ⅓ cup very cold water, or as needed |
| 1 teaspoon baking powder | |

1. Preheat oven to 350°F. Spray baking sheet with nonstick cooking spray.

2. In large bowl, combine flours, wheat germ, garlic, sugar, baking powder, pepper, and salt.

3. In small bowl, combine yogurt and oil. Add to flour mixture, stirring. Gradually add water until mixture forms a dough. Knead slightly until it forms a mass.

4. Roll out dough until $1/16$ inch thick. Cut with knife or pastry cutter into 2-inch squares. Halve squares into triangles.

5. Place triangles on prepared baking sheet. Bake until golden brown, about 10 minutes. Cool on rack.

| Calories: | 151 | Cholesterol: | .7 mg | Vitamin A: | 8 IU |
|-----------|-----|--------------|-------|------------|------|
| Fat: | 4 gm | Sodium: | 326 mg | Vitamin C: | 1 mg |
| Sat. fat: | .5 gm | Fiber: | 2.6 gm | Zinc: | 1.5 mg |
| Iron: | 1.7 mg | Cal. from fat: 24% | | | |

# Marinated Vegetables

• A carefully arranged platter of these marinated vegetables make a stunning addition to a buffet. Choose whatever vegetables you like, keeping in mind how the colors will look together on a plate. Remember, variety is the key.

Preparation time: 10 minutes, plus at least 1 hour marination

Cooking time: 6 minutes

Serves 5

| | |
|---|---|
| 3 medium carrots, peeled and cut in sticks | ¼ cup white wine vinegar |
| ½ small cabbage, cut lengthwise in 6 to 8 wedges | 4 cloves garlic, crushed with flat side of knife |
| 1 red or yellow bell pepper, seeded and cut in wide strips | 2 tablespoons coarsely chopped fresh oregano leaves |
| 1 small fennel bulb, cut in wedges | 1 tablespoon extra virgin olive oil |
| 5 Hungarian hot peppers (see note) | 1 teaspoon sugar |

1. Place carrots, cabbage, bell pepper, fennel, and hot peppers in a covered steamer basket over 1 inch gently boiling water. Steam until just tender, about 6 minutes.

2. Meanwhile, in shallow baking dish, combine vinegar, garlic, oregano, oil, and sugar. Add warm vegetables and marinate until room temperature at least 1 hour, or overnight, covered with plastic wrap.

## Note:

Hungarian hot peppers are medium-hot long peppers. They can be replaced by any other pepper, hot or sweet.

| Calories: | 90 | Cholesterol: | 0 | Vitamin A: | 10,605 IU |
|---|---|---|---|---|---|
| Fat: | 3.2 gm | Sodium: | 58 mg | Vitamin C: | 170 mg |
| Sat. fat: | .4 gm | Fiber: | 3.7 gm | Zinc: | .3 mg |
| Iron: | 1.6 mg | Cal. from fat: | 31% | | |

# Tomato Crostini

• Make this dish in summer when tomatoes are at their peak, bursting with juice and flavor, and fresh basil is abundant.

Preparation time: 10 minutes

Marination time: 1 to 2 hours

Serves 4

| | |
|---|---|
| 4 medium tomatoes, diced (4 cups) | 2 cloves garlic, minced |
| 1 cup very thinly sliced red onion | ½ teaspoon freshly ground black pepper |
| 1 cup (packed) fresh basil leaves, chopped | Salt, to taste (optional) |
| 2 tablespoons red wine vinegar | 4 thick slices whole-grain bread |
| 1 tablespoon extra virgin olive oil, or more to taste | 1 clove garlic, peeled and halved |

1.  In large bowl, combine tomatoes, onion, basil, vinegar, olive oil, garlic, pepper, and salt (if used). Cover and marinate at room temperature 1 to 2 hours. Do not refrigerate.

2.  Toast or broil bread until well browned. Rub each piece with halved garlic. Place on serving plates and top with tomato mixture.

### Nutrients Per Serving

| | | | | | |
|---|---|---|---|---|---|
| Calories: | 174 | Cholesterol: | 0 | Vitamin A: | 1,667 IU |
| Fat: | 5.4 gm | Sodium: | 161 mg | Vitamin C: | 43 mg |
| Sat. fat: | .8 gm | Fiber: | 5 gm | Zinc: | .8 mg |
| Iron: | 4.5 mg | Cal. from fat: | 28% | | |

# Sweet and Hot Pepper Crostini

• This is a great first course or light lunch. We've specified Italian frying peppers (sometimes called simply Italian peppers), but experiment with different types of peppers, including hot Hungarian peppers, jalapeños, or any of the rainbow of varieties available in the summer. Choose peppers with different amounts of heat according to your taste.

Preparation time: 10 minutes

Cooking time: 20 minutes

Serves 4

| | |
|---|---|
| 2 teaspoons olive oil | 1 poblano pepper, seeded and diced |
| 4 cloves garlic, peeled and crushed with flat side of knife | 1 tablespoon fresh rosemary leaves, chopped |
| 2 Italian frying peppers, seeded and diced | Freshly ground black pepper, to taste |
| 1 red bell pepper, seeded and diced | Salt, to taste (optional) |
| 1 yellow bell pepper, seeded and diced | ¼ cup chopped Italian (flat-leaf) parsley leaves |
| | 4 thick slices whole-grain bread |

**1.** In large nonstick skillet, heat oil over medium heat. Add garlic and cook, stirring, until lightly browned, about 5 minutes.

**2.** Add peppers and continue cooking, covered, until soft, 10 to 15 minutes. Stir in rosemary, pepper, and salt (if used). Remove from heat. Toss peppers with parsley.

**3.** Meanwhile, toast bread until well browned. Place on serving plate and top with pepper mixture.

*continued*

## Nutrients Per Serving

| | | | | | |
|---|---|---|---|---|---|
| Calories: | 125 | Cholesterol: | 0 | Vitamin A: | 1,710 IU |
| Fat: | 3.5 gm | Sodium: | 144 mg | Vitamin C: | 162 mg |
| Sat. fat: | .5 gm | Fiber: | 3.2 gm | Zinc: | .5 mg |
| Iron: | 2 mg | Cal. from fat: | 25% | | |

# Avocado and Tomato Salsa

• This is a combination of two healthy classics, guacamole and Mexican salsa. Try serving it as an appetizer salad on lettuce leaves or as an hors d'oeuvre with tortilla chips, Whole-Wheat Garlic Chips (page 52), or fresh vegetable crudités.

### Note:

Don't be too concerned about the fat content of this recipe. The percentage of fat calories seems high because the calorie content is quite low. Besides, an appetizer portion contains less than 1 gram of saturated fat.

Preparation time: 15 minutes

Cooking time: None

Serves 6 as an hors d'oeuvre, or 4 as an appetizer

| | |
|---|---|
| 1 ripe avocado, peeled, seeded, and diced | 1 clove garlic, minced |
| 1 large tomato, diced (1½ cups) | ¼ cup (packed) fresh cilantro leaves, chopped |
| ½ cup diced yellow bell pepper | 1 teaspoon freshly ground black pepper |
| ¾ cup finely diced red onion | Salt, to taste (optional) |
| 2 tablespoons fresh lime juice | |
| 1 jalapeño pepper, seeded and minced | |

1.   In large bowl, combine avocado, tomato, bell pepper, onion, juice, jalapeño, garlic, cilantro, pepper, and salt (if used). Stir well.

2.   Serve promptly.

*continued*

## Nutrients Per Hors d'oeuvre Serving

| Calories: | 78 | Cholesterol: | 0 mg | Vitamin A: | 586 IU |
|---|---|---|---|---|---|
| Fat: | 5.3 gm | Sodium: | 11 mg | Vitamin C: | 27 mg |
| Sat. fat: | .8 gm | Fiber: | 1.8 gm | Zinc: | trace |
| Iron: | .8 mg | Cal. from fat: | 62% | | |

**Chapter 5**

# Breakfast Foods and Drinks

With breakfast often considered the most important meal of the day, it can't hurt to jump start your antioxidant-rich eating scheme with some morning heavy hitters. A one-two punch of both wheat germ and walnuts boosts the vitamin E content of the Raspberry-Walnut Muffins, fragrant, nutty-tasting treats that contain a colorful and sweet red pocket of fruit preserves in their centers. And Pumpkin-Nut Quick Bread, with its rich supply of beta-carotene and healthy dose of vitamin E, is one of those easy-to-freeze baked goods that come in handy for unexpected company and family "snack attacks" all year long. When you're ready to break out of the boxed cereal rut, you'll find the Oatmeal Buttermilk Pancakes offer a tasty way to obtain small amounts of vitamin E and a hefty dose of beta-carotene, while Molasses-Nut Granola offers lots of fiber and some vitamin E.

# Oatmeal Buttermilk Pancakes with Mango Maple Syrup

- It is easy to replace premade pancake mix with this homemade version, and it is well worth it. These pancakes will make a delicious part of a vitamin-rich and low-fat breakfast.

Preparation time: 10 minutes

Cooking time: 5 to 6 minutes each

Makes about eight 5-inch pancakes

| | |
|---|---|
| ¾ cup rolled oats (not instant) | 1 teaspoon baking soda |
| ½ cup unbleached all-purpose flour | 1 cup buttermilk |
| 3 tablespoons wheat germ | 1 large egg, separated |
| 2 tablespoons sugar | 1 large egg white |
| 1 tablespoon grated lemon zest | 3 cups mango slices |
| 1½ teaspoons baking powder | ¼ cup pure maple syrup |

**1.** In food processor, grind oats to coarse crumbs. Transfer to medium mixing bowl. Add flour, wheat germ, sugar, zest, baking powder, and baking soda. Stir well.

**2.** In separate bowl, whisk together buttermilk and egg yolk. Pour over dry ingredients. Mix until just combined. In clean bowl, beat egg whites until soft peaks form. Gently fold into batter.

**3.** Heat griddle or large nonstick skillet over medium heat. Spray with nonstick cooking spray. Drop ¼ cup of the batter onto hot surface, spreading mixture to 4 to 5 inches. Cook until top is bubbly, about 3 minutes. Flip over and cook until underside is golden, about 3 minutes. Continue with remaining batter, keeping cooked pancakes warm in low oven.

*continued*

**4.** Serve pancakes sprinkled with 1 cup mango slices and drizzled with mango maple syrup, made by pureeing remaining 2 cups mango slices with ¼ cup maple syrup in food processor.

### Nutrients Per 1-Pancake Serving

| | | | | | |
|---|---|---|---|---|---|
| Calories: | 173 | Cholesterol: | 28 mg | Vitamin A: | 3,021 IU |
| Fat: | 2.4 gm | Sodium: | 298 mg | Vitamin C: | 24 mg |
| Sat. fat: | .5 gm | Fiber: | 2 gm | Zinc: | .9 mg |
| Iron: | 1.3 mg | Cal. from fat: | 12% | | |

# Molasses-Nut Granola

• Homemade granola? Of course. The best part about making your own granola is that you can choose your own ingredients. This recipe is the super-antioxidant mixture. Modify ingredients to your taste, but try to keep the healthy basics.

Serve plain as a snack or with low-fat milk.

Preparation time: 10 minutes

Cooking time: 20 to 25 minutes

Makes 3 cups

| | |
|---|---|
| 2 cups rolled oats (not instant) | ¼ cup molasses |
| ½ cup diced dried apricots (3 ounces) | ¼ cup honey |
| ½ cup slivered almonds | 1 tablespoon safflower oil |
| ½ teaspoon ground cinnamon | 3 tablespoons wheat germ |
| Pinch grated nutmeg | ¼ cup raisins |

**1.** Preheat oven to 350°F.

**2.** In large bowl, combine oats, apricots, almonds, cinnamon, and nutmeg. Set aside.

**3.** In small saucepan, heat molasses, honey, and oil over low heat until they liquefy. Pour into the oat mixture. Toss gently until completely coated. Sprinkle with wheat germ.

**4.** Pour the mixture onto a jelly-roll pan and bake, tossing occasionally, until golden brown, 20 to 25 minutes. Add raisins and toss. Cool. Store in an airtight container for up to 1 month.

*continued*

## Nutrients Per ½-cup Serving

| Calories: | 325 | Cholesterol: | 0 | Vitamin A: | 1,055 IU |
|-----------|-----|--------------|---|-----------|----------|
| Fat: | 9.4 gm | Sodium: | 10 mg | Vitamin C: | 1 mg |
| Sat. fat: | 1 gm | Fiber: | 5.1 gm | Zinc: | 1.8 mg |
| Iron: | 3.3 mg | Cal. from fat: | 26% | | |

# Hot Wheatberry Cereal

- Try this cereal for vitamin E, selenium, and fiber. A great alternative to oatmeal, enjoy it for its nutty taste and chewy texture.

Preparation time: 5 minutes

Cooking time: 35 to 40 minutes

Serves 6

| | |
|---|---|
| 1½ cups wheatberries | 4 dried apricots, chopped |
| ¾ cup low-fat (1%) milk | Pinch salt |
| 3 tablespoons (packed) light brown sugar | ⅓ cup sliced almonds (optional), gently crushed |

1. Simmer wheatberries in plenty of water until tender, 30 minutes. Drain well.

2. In medium saucepan, combine wheatberries and milk. Bring to a boil, reduce heat to low, and simmer 5 minutes. Add sugar, apricots, and salt. Continue cooking until sugar is dissolved. Remove from heat and stir in almonds (if used). Serve hot.

### Nutrients Per Serving

| Calories: | 191 | Cholesterol: | 2 mg | Vitamin A: | 231 IU |
|---|---|---|---|---|---|
| Fat: | 1.8 gm | Sodium: | 65 mg | Vitamin C: | <1 mg |
| Sat. fat: | .2 gm | Fiber: | 4 gm | Zinc: | .3 mg |
| Iron: | 2.3 mg | Cal. from fat: | 9% | | |

# Raspberry-Walnut Muffins

• These nutty-flavored muffins have an authentic homemade look with their ruby dimples of raspberry. More important, however, is that they are packed with vitamin E.

Preparation time: 15 minutes

Cooking time: 25 minutes

Makes 12 muffins

| | |
|---|---|
| 1 cup unbleached all-purpose flour | 1 teaspoon baking soda |
| ½ cup whole-wheat flour | ½ teaspoon salt |
| ½ cup (packed) light brown sugar | 1 cup buttermilk |
| ¼ cup granulated sugar | ¼ cup safflower oil |
| ⅓ cup wheat germ | 1 large egg |
| ¼ cup chopped walnuts | 1 teaspoon pure vanilla extract |
| 2 teaspoons baking powder | ½ cup raspberry spreadable fruit |

1.  Preheat oven to 400°F. Spray 12 muffin cups with nonstick cooking spray.

2.  In large bowl, combine flours, sugars, wheat germ, walnuts, baking powder, baking soda, and salt. Stir well. In separate bowl, whisk together buttermilk, oil, egg, and vanilla.

3.  Pour liquid ingredients over dry. Stir just until blended. Pour mixture into prepared cups.

4.  With a finger, make a wide indentation in each muffin. Fill with 1 rounded teaspoon spreadable fruit. Bake 25 minutes. Cool in pan on rack.

## Nutrients Per Serving

| | | | | | |
|---|---|---|---|---|---|
| Calories: | 232 | Cholesterol: | 19 mg | Vitamin A: | 36 IU |
| Fat: | 5.1 gm | Sodium: | 309 mg | Vitamin C: | <1 mg |
| Sat. fat: | .6 gm | Fiber: | 1.4 gm | Zinc: | .9 mg |
| Iron: | 1.4 mg | Cal. from fat: | 20% | | |

# Double-Apricot Oatmeal Muffins

- Double apricot means double beta-carotene. These muffins are made with no fat—the apricot puree keeps them moist. They will quickly become favorites with your family as they have with mine.

Preparation time: 10 minutes

Baking time: 20 minutes

Makes 12 muffins

| | |
|---|---|
| 1 16-ounce can apricots packed in juice, drained | ¼ cup sugar |
| 1 cup unbleached all-purpose flour | 2 teaspoons grated lemon zest |
| ½ cup whole-wheat flour | 2 teaspoons baking powder |
| ½ cup rolled oats (not instant) | 1 teaspoon baking soda |
| ½ cup chopped dried apricots (3 ounces) | ½ teaspoon salt |
| | 1 large egg |
| | 1 teaspoon pure vanilla extract |

1. Preheat oven to 400°F. Spray 12 muffin cups with nonstick cooking spray.

2. Puree canned apricots until smooth. Measure 1 cup, reserve remaining puree for another purpose.

3. In large bowl, combine flours, oats, dried apricots, sugar, zest, baking powder, baking soda, and salt. Stir well. In separate bowl, whisk together 1 cup apricot puree, egg, and vanilla.

4. Pour liquid ingredients over dry. Stir just until blended. Pour mixture into prepared cups.

5. Bake 20 minutes. Cool in pan on wire rack.

| Calories: | 148 | Cholesterol: | 18 mg | Vitamin A: | 1,182 IU |
|---|---|---|---|---|---|
| Fat: | 3.5 gm | Sodium: | 286 mg | Vitamin C: | 2 mg |
| Sat. fat: | .4 gm | Fiber: | 1.9 gm | Zinc: | <1 mg |
| Iron: | 1.4 mg | Cal. from fat: | 21% | | |

# Pumpkin-Nut Quick Bread

• This pumpkin bread is a healthy morning treat or afternoon snack. Each slice is packed with vitamins A and E. How could something so delicious be so healthy?

Preparation time: 10 minutes

Cooking time: 1 hour 15 minutes

Serves 10

| | |
|---|---|
| 1½ cups unbleached all-purpose flour | ½ teaspoon ground allspice |
| ¼ cup whole-wheat flour | ½ teaspoon ground cinnamon |
| ½ cup chopped walnuts | ¼ teaspoon ground cloves |
| ½ cup raisins | ¼ teaspoon grated nutmeg |
| ⅓ cup sugar | 1 cup pumpkin puree, canned or homemade |
| ⅓ cup wheat germ | |
| 2½ teaspoons baking powder | 1 large egg |
| 1 teaspoon baking soda | 1 large egg white |
| 2 teaspoons grated orange zest | 1 teaspoon pure vanilla extract |
| ½ teaspoon salt | |

**1.** Preheat oven to 350°F. Spray 9×5-inch loaf pan with nonstick cooking spray. Sprinkle with flour. Shake off excess.

**2.** In large bowl, combine flours, walnuts, raisins, sugar, wheat germ, baking powder, baking soda, zest, salt, and spices. Stir well. In separate bowl, whisk together pumpkin puree, egg, egg white, and vanilla.

**3.** Pour liquid ingredients over dry. Stir just until blended. Pour mixture into prepared pan.

4. Bake 1 hour 15 minutes, until toothpick inserted in center comes out clean. Cool in pan on wire rack.

| Calories: | 197 | Cholesterol: | 21 mg | Vitamin A: | 6,000 IU |
|---|---|---|---|---|---|
| Fat: | 5 gm | Sodium: | 368 mg | Vitamin C: | 2 mg |
| Sat. fat: | .6 gm | Fiber: | 2 gm | Zinc: | 1 mg |
| Iron: | 2 mg | Cal. from fat: | 25% | | |

# Strawberry-Mango Shake

- This creamy, calcium-rich shake is an easy, refreshing way to add some vitamins to your diet. With a muffin or whole-grain bread, the shake will make a perfect breakfast. Drink it alone as an afternoon snack. Choose ripe sweet fruit and you won't need any added sugar.

Preparation time: 5 minutes

Cooking time: None

Serves 2

| | |
|---|---|
| 1 pint strawberries | 1 tablespoon chopped fresh mint leaves |
| 1 mango, peeled, pitted, and cut in chunks | 5 ice cubes |
| 1 cup plain low-fat yogurt | 1 to 2 teaspoons sugar (optional) |

Combine strawberries, mango, yogurt, mint, and ice in blender or food processor. Pulse until well combined and ice is crushed. Add sugar (if used). Serve in tall glasses.

### Nutrients Per Serving

| | | | | | |
|---|---|---|---|---|---|
| Calories: | 187 | Cholesterol: | 7 mg | Vitamin A: | 4,212 IU |
| Fat: | 2.6 gm | Sodium: | 85 mg | Vitamin C: | 120 mg |
| Sat. fat: | 1.2 gm | Fiber: | 5.3 gm | Zinc: | 1.2 mg |
| Iron: | <1 mg | Cal. from fat: | 13% | | |

# Tropical Citrus Shake

- Welcome to the islands! Shakes like this one are very popular in the Caribbean, but you can drink it at home, without the airfare. With double the RDA for vitamin C, it is a refreshing cool-down for the sweltering summer months.

Preparation time: 5 minutes

Cooking time: None

Serves 2

| | |
|---|---|
| 1 papaya, peeled, seeded, and cut into chunks | ¼ cup fresh lime juice |
| 1 persimmon, peeled and cored | 1½ teaspoons grated fresh ginger |
| ½ cup orange juice, fresh or from concentrate | 6 ice cubes |

Combine papaya, persimmon, juices, ginger, and ice in blender or food processor. Pulse until well combined and ice is crushed. Serve in tall glasses.

### Nutrients Per Serving

| Calories: | 111 | Cholesterol: | 0 | Vitamin A: | 3,115 IU |
|---|---|---|---|---|---|
| Fat: | .4 gm | Sodium: | 10 mg | Vitamin C: | 128 mg |
| Sat. fat: | tr | Fiber: | 1.5 gm | Zinc: | .1 mg |
| Iron: | .6 mg | Cal. from fat: | 3% | | |

# Bitter Orange and Apricot Marmalade

• Here is a nutritious alternative to sugary jams. It is an easy way to spread a few extra vitamins on your morning toast. If you like a smoother spread, try pureeing the warm mixture.

Preparation time: 20 minutes

Cooking time: 25 minutes

Makes 3 cups

| | |
|---|---|
| 1 cup dried apricots (6 ounces) | 2 tablespoons finely shredded orange zest, orange part only |
| 2 cups orange juice, fresh or from concentrate | 2 tablespoons finely shredded lemon zest, yellow part only |
| ¼ cup fresh lemon juice | |
| 1 cup water | |

**1.** Thinly slice apricots, smaller than ⅛ inch. Place in a medium saucepan. Add juices, water, and zests.

**2.** Heat mixture to boiling, then reduce heat to low and simmer until apricots are soft and liquid is syrupy, about 25 minutes. Transfer to a bowl and cool, then cover and refrigerate.

### Nutrients Per Tablespoon

| Calories: | 14 | Cholesterol: | 0 | Vitamin A: | 266 IU |
|---|---|---|---|---|---|
| Fat: | tr | Sodium: | <1 mg | Vitamin C: | 5 mg |
| Sat. fat: | 0 | Fiber: | .3 gm | Zinc: | tr |
| Iron: | .2 mg | Cal. from fat: | trace | | |

Chapter 6

........................

# Soups

Winter or summer, hearty soups are perfect as meal starters. Or why not pair a soup rich in beta-carotene like Spicy Curried Carrot with a whole-grain bread for a complete and satisfying meal? Silky smooth Basil–Red Pepper Soup manages to deliver whopping amounts of both beta-carotene and vitamin C, while carrying only 41 calories per serving and virtually no fat. Besides offering an astounding amount of beta-carotene, the Chicken Barley Soup packs nine grams of fiber per serving, or about half of your daily fiber needs! In the hot summer months, you'll want to sip on a cool batch of the strawberry soup, made special with a splash of balsamic vinegar. It carries both a hefty dose of fiber and vitamin C, all delivered in an elegant, delicious package. Indeed, when you crave soup, you'll appreciate the wide range of tastes and textures that deliver antioxidants in so many different ways.

# Rich Tomato-Cabbage Soup

• This soup makes a rich, delicious winter lunch, accented with the homey flavors of Eastern Europe. Serve it with a thick slice of whole-grain bread.

Preparation time: 10 minutes

Cooking time: 40 minutes

Serves 4

| | |
|---|---|
| 1 tablespoon olive oil | 2 cups low-sodium chicken or beef broth, canned or homemade |
| 1 cup chopped onion | |
| ½ cup chopped carrot | 3 tablespoons chopped fresh rosemary leaves |
| ½ cup chopped celery | |
| 3 cloves garlic, chopped | 1 piece (2½ × 1 inch) orange peel |
| ½ head (1 pound) green cabbage, chopped (4 cups) | 1 bay leaf |
| 1 can (28 ounces) whole plum tomatoes, chopped, reserve juice | |

**1.** In large (6-quart) saucepan or Dutch oven, heat oil over medium heat. Add onion, carrot, celery, and garlic; cook until wilted, about 8 minutes.

**2.** Add cabbage, tomatoes and juice, broth, rosemary, orange peel, and bay leaf. Simmer 30 minutes. Let soup rest 5 minutes before serving.

### Nutrients Per Serving

| | | | | | |
|---|---|---|---|---|---|
| Calories: | 180 | Cholesterol: | 8 mg | Vitamin A: | 5,266 IU |
| Fat: | 5.25 gm | Sodium: | 417 mg | Vitamin C: | 94 mg |
| Sat. fat: | 1.2 gm | Fiber: | 5.6 gm | Zinc: | .8 mg |
| Iron: | 2.8 mg | Cal. from fat: | 26% | | |

# Creamy Broccoli Soup

• This version of broccoli soup is much lighter and brighter than what we are all used to. I've made it without all the fat of the classic cream-based soup, and I've added lots of fresh herbs to wake up the flavor.

Preparation time: 20 minutes

Cooking time: 10 minutes

Serves 4

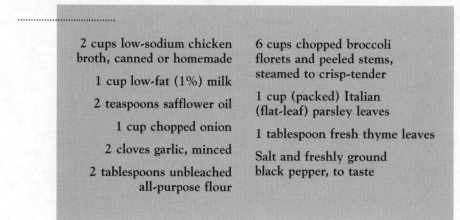

2 cups low-sodium chicken broth, canned or homemade

1 cup low-fat (1%) milk

2 teaspoons safflower oil

1 cup chopped onion

2 cloves garlic, minced

2 tablespoons unbleached all-purpose flour

6 cups chopped broccoli florets and peeled stems, steamed to crisp-tender

1 cup (packed) Italian (flat-leaf) parsley leaves

1 tablespoon fresh thyme leaves

Salt and freshly ground black pepper, to taste

**1.** In small saucepan, heat stock and milk until almost simmering. Meanwhile, in large (3-quart) saucepan, heat oil over medium heat. Add onion and garlic and cook until translucent. Add flour and cook, stirring, 1 minute. Add hot broth and milk and simmer, stirring constantly with whisk, until mixture thickens, about 5 minutes. Remove from heat and cool slightly.

**2.** Carefully transfer mixture to food processor, 2 to 3 cups at a time. Add broccoli, parsley, and thyme. Puree until smooth, in batches as necessary.

**3.** Return soup to pan and reheat just to boiling. Season with salt and pepper to taste.

| Calories: | 132 | Cholesterol: | 2 mg | Vitamin A: | 3,146 IU |
|-----------|-----|--------------|------|-----------|----------|
| Fat: | 4 gm | Sodium: | 395 mg | Vitamin C: | 144 mg |
| Sat. fat: | .7 gm | Fiber: | 5.3 gm | Zinc: | 1 mg |
| Iron: | 3 mg | Cal. from fat: | 20% | | |

# Kale Soup with Rice and Lemon

- If you like lemon, you will love this soup, which is rich in fiber, vitamin A, and vitamin C. Its crisp flavors are characteristic of Mediterranean cuisine.

Preparation time: 15 minutes

Cooking time: 35 minutes

Serves 4

2 cups low-sodium chicken broth, canned or homemade

2 cups water

2 teaspoons olive oil

1 cup chopped onion

8 ounces kale, thick stalks removed and chopped (4 cups packed)

½ cup brown rice

¼ cup lemon juice

1 teaspoon grated lemon zest

½ teaspoon freshly ground black pepper, or to taste

1. In medium-size saucepan, bring broth and water to boil. In large (3 quart) saucepan, heat oil over medium heat. Add onion and cook until translucent, 5 to 6 minutes.

2. Add broth, kale, rice, juice, and zest to pot. Bring to boil, reduce heat to low, and simmer, covered, 30 minutes or until rice is tender. Add pepper to taste.

## Nutrients Per Serving

| | | | | | |
|---|---|---|---|---|---|
| Calories: | 165 | Cholesterol: | 0 | Vitamin A: | 3,134 IU |
| Fat: | 4.4 gm | Sodium: | 661 mg | Vitamin C: | 49 mg |
| Sat. fat: | .5 gm | Fiber: | 3.8 gm | Zinc: | .7 mg |
| Iron: | 1 mg | Cal. from fat: | 24% | | |

# Chicken-Barley Soup

• Here is a healthy version of the classic dish, with a whopping dose of beta-carotene, vitamin A, and fiber. This soup gets most of its flavor from the vegetables and the bright flavor of fresh herbs, not to mention vitamin C from parsley and selenium from barley.

Preparation time: 15 minutes

Cooking time: 40 minutes, plus 5 minutes resting time

Serves 4

| | |
|---|---|
| 6 cups water | 1 bay leaf |
| 4 chicken thighs, skin and fat removed | ½ cup (packed) Italian (flat-leaf) parsley leaves, chopped |
| 4 cups 1-inch pieces peeled carrots | 2 teaspoons chopped fresh rosemary leaves |
| 1 cup diced onion | ½ teaspoon freshly ground black pepper |
| 1 cup diced celery | |
| ½ cup barley | Salt, to taste (optional) |
| 4 cloves garlic, minced | |

**1.** In large (6-quart) saucepan, combine water, chicken, carrots, onion, celery, barley, garlic, and bay leaf. Bring to boil, then reduce heat to low and simmer, uncovered, until chicken is tender, about 40 minutes.

**2.** Remove chicken from pot. Separate chicken from bone and tear into strips. Meanwhile, allow soup to rest, covered, off heat at least 5 minutes.

**3.** Stir in parsley, rosemary, pepper, and salt (if using). Return chicken to saucepan. The soup can be served right away or the next day.

*continued*

## Nutrients Per Serving

| | | | | | |
|---|---|---|---|---|---|
| Calories: | 240 | Cholesterol: | 57 mg | Vitamin A: | 31,437 IU |
| Fat: | 3.6 gm | Sodium: | 132 mg | Vitamin C: | 25 mg |
| Sat. fat: | <1 gm | Fiber: | 9 gm | Zinc: | 2.3 mg |
| Iron: | 3 mg | Cal. from fat: | 14% | | |

# Potato-Fish Chowder

• This selenium-rich soup is a light and stylish version of fish chowder. Pieces of fish are poached in a smooth potato broth. Serve it as a first course or use twice as much fish for a main course. I usually buy a whole fish, fillet it, and make broth from the head and bones. Try it when you have the time, or stick with this quicker version.

Preparation time: 10 minutes

Cooking time: 30 minutes

Serves 4

1 pound potatoes, peeled and cut into 2-inch pieces (2½ cups)

1 cup chopped onion

5 cloves garlic, quartered

3 cups water

2 cups clam juice

¾ cup whole milk

½ cup (packed) Italian (flat-leaf) parsley leaves

1 teaspoon fresh lemon juice

¼ teaspoon grated nutmeg

12 ounces fish fillet, preferably bass or red snapper, cut in 1-inch pieces

**1.** In large (3-quart) saucepan, combine potatoes, onion, garlic, and water. Bring to boil, then reduce heat to low and simmer until potatoes are tender, about 20 minutes. Drain well.

**2.** In two batches, transfer potatoes to food processor, along with the clam juice, milk, parsley, lemon juice, and nutmeg. Puree until smooth. Return mixture to pot.

**3.** Heat soup until almost boiling. Add fish and cook gently until cooked through, 3 to 4 minutes. Serve promptly.

*continued*

## Nutrients Per Serving

| | | | | | |
|---|---|---|---|---|---|
| Calories: | 199 | Cholesterol: | 43 mg | Vitamin A: | 583 IU |
| Fat: | 2.3 gm | Sodium: | 338 mg | Vitamin C: | 32 mg |
| Sat. fat: | 1.1 gm | Fiber: | 2.5 gm | Zinc: | 1 mg |
| Iron: | 1.8 mg | Cal. from fat: | 11% | | |

# Spicy Curried Carrot Soup

• This soup is a sensational way to start a meal. It is sure to wake up your tastebuds without filling you up. If you want a little less spice, the chili pepper can be removed after 10 minutes.

Preparation time: 15 minutes

Cooking time: 30 minutes

Serves 6

2 pounds carrots, peeled and cut in 1-inch pieces (about 6 cups)

5 cups low-sodium chicken broth, canned or homemade

1 dried hot chili pepper, any type

4 teaspoons minced fresh ginger

3 cloves garlic

1 teaspoon curry powder

1 teaspoon ground cumin

½ teaspoon freshly ground black pepper

3 tablespoons chopped fresh cilantro leaves

1. In large (5-quart) saucepan, combine carrots, broth, hot pepper, ginger, garlic, curry powder, cumin, and black pepper. Bring mixture to a boil, then reduce heat to low and simmer 30 minutes or until carrots are tender.

2. Transfer mixture to food processor, 2 to 3 cups at a time. Puree until smooth.

3. Return soup to saucepan and reheat. Stir in cilantro. Serve promptly.

| Nutrients Per Serving | | | | | |
|---|---|---|---|---|---|
| Calories: | 91 | Cholesterol: | 0 | Vitamin A: | 42,713 IU |
| Fat: | 1.4 gm | Sodium: | 588 mg | Vitamin C: | 15 mg |
| Sat. fat: | tr | Fiber: | 5 gm | Zinc: | .3 mg |
| Iron: | 1.2 mg | Cal. from fat: | 14% | | |

# Basil–Red Pepper Soup

• In this simple but delicate soup, crisp red bell peppers are transformed into a silky puree flecked with fresh basil. For a golden treat, make it with yellow peppers instead.

Preparation time: 5 minutes

Cooking time: 25 minutes

Serves 4

5 large red bell peppers, seeded and cut in 1-inch pieces

3 cloves garlic, quartered

2½ cups water

¼ cup (packed) fresh basil leaves, chopped

1 teaspoon red wine vinegar, or more to taste

2 teaspoons extra virgin olive oil (optional)

Salt and freshly ground black pepper, to taste

**1.** In medium (2-quart) saucepan, combine peppers, garlic, and water. Bring to boil, then reduce heat to low and simmer, covered, until tender, about 25 minutes.

**2.** Using slotted spoon, transfer solids to food processor. Puree until smooth, adding cooking liquid until mixture reaches desired consistency. Discard extra cooking liquid. Return soup to pan.

**3.** Heat soup to serving temperature. Stir in basil, vinegar, optional olive oil, pepper, and salt to serve.

## Nutrients Per Serving

| Calories: | 41 | Cholesterol: | 0 | Vitamin A: | 7,257 IU |
|---|---|---|---|---|---|
| Fat: | .3 gm | Sodium: | 3 mg | Vitamin C: | 239 mg |
| Sat. fat: | tr | Fiber: | 2 gm | Zinc: | <1 mg |
| Iron: | 1 mg | Cal. from fat: | 7% | | |

# Butternut Squash and Orange Soup

• When you taste this soup, you certainly will not be thinking about vitamins—just the smooth texture and subtle flavors. But don't be fooled—this one is loaded with beta-carotene.

Preparation time: 10 minutes

Cooking time: 15 minutes

Serves 4

1 butternut squash (2 pounds), peeled and cut in 1-inch chunks (3½ cups)

1½ cups low-sodium chicken broth, canned or homemade

½ teaspoon ground coriander

½ teaspoon cayenne pepper

2 tablespoons orange juice, fresh or from concentrate

2 tablespoons chopped Italian (flat-leaf) parsley or cilantro

1 clove garlic, minced

1 teaspoon grated orange zest

¼ teaspoon freshly ground black pepper

**1.** In medium (2-quart) saucepan, combine squash, broth, coriander, and cayenne. Bring to boil, then reduce heat to low and simmer until tender, 10 to 15 minutes

**2.** Transfer mixture to food processor. Add juice and process until smooth. Return to pan.

**3.** Just before serving, chop together parsley or cilantro, garlic, zest, and pepper. Heat soup until almost boiling. Pour into serving bowls and sprinkle with zest mixture.

### Nutrients Per Serving

| Calories: | 101 | Cholesterol: | 0 | Vitamin A: | 15,070 IU |
|-----------|-----|--------------|---|------------|-----------|
| Fat: | .6 gm | Sodium: | 249 mg | Vitamin C: | 46 mg |
| Sat. fat: | tr | Fiber: | 3.9 gm | Zinc: | .3 mg |
| Iron: | 1.5 mg | Cal. from fat: 5% | | | |

# Spinach-Dill Soup

• Spinach soup does not have to be made with cream. In this version, the bright green flavors of spinach and dill come through in the fresh-tasting puree.

Preparation time: 8 minutes

Cooking time: 10 minutes

Serves 4

| | |
|---|---|
| 1 tablespoon extra virgin olive oil | 1 cup diced cooked potato |
| 4 cloves garlic, minced | ¼ cup chopped fresh dill |
| 6 cups (packed) spinach leaves (1 pound), well rinsed | ½ teaspoon salt (optional) |
| 2 cups low-sodium chicken broth, canned or homemade | ½ teaspoon freshly ground black pepper |

**1.** In large nonstick skillet, heat oil over medium heat. Add garlic and cook until just wilted. Add spinach, increase heat to high, and cook, tossing, until very soft, about 5 minutes.

**2.** Transfer spinach to food processor along with broth. Puree until very smooth, 3 to 4 minutes.

**3.** Add potato, dill, salt (if used), and pepper. Puree until just smooth. Add water to desired consistency.

**4.** Reheat soup just before serving.

## Nutrients Per Serving

| | | | | | |
|---|---|---|---|---|---|
| Calories: | 117 | Cholesterol: | 0 | Vitamin A: | 7,622 IU |
| Fat: | 4.4 gm | Sodium: | 414 mg | Vitamin C: | 36 mg |
| Sat. fat: | .5 gm | Fiber: | 3.6 gm | Zinc: | .7 mg |
| Iron: | 3.7 mg | Cal. from fat: | 34% | | |

# Spicy Summer Tomato Soup

• Try serving this cool gazpacho in tall glasses as a drink. The amount of vinegar that you will need will vary with the acidity of the tomatoes. Add a little at a time, tasting as you go.

Preparation time: 15 minutes

Cooking time: None

Serves 4

2 pounds very ripe tomatoes, cut into chunks (about 5 cups)

1 cup peeled and cubed cucumber

½ cup cubed green pepper

½ cup chopped red onion

3 tablespoons chopped fresh cilantro

2 teaspoons seeded and minced jalapeño pepper

1 clove garlic, minced

1 tablespoon red wine vinegar, or more to taste

Salt, to taste (optional)

1.  Combine tomato, cucumber, green pepper, onion, cilantro, jalapeño, and garlic in food processor. Puree until chunky smooth.

2.  Stir in vinegar and salt (if used). Chill if desired, but the consistency is better at room temperature.

### Nutrients Per Serving

| | | | | | |
|---|---|---|---|---|---|
| Calories: | 66 | Cholesterol: | 0 | Vitamin A: | 1,534 IU |
| Fat: | .8 gm | Sodium: | 25 mg | Vitamin C: | 64 mg |
| Sat. fat: | .1 gm | Fiber: | 3.6 gm | Zinc: | .2 mg |
| Iron: | 1.3 mg | Cal. from fat: | 11% | | |

# Cold Strawberry Soup with Balsamic Vinegar

• This is an excellent palate cleanser at the end of a meal, or between courses at a formal dinner. It will be best at the peak of strawberry season and if you use a high-quality balsamic vinegar.

Preparation time: 5 minutes

Cooking time: 18 minutes

Serves 4

| | |
|---|---|
| 2 pints ripe strawberries | 2 teaspoons cornstarch, mixed with 2 tablespoons water |
| 1 cup red wine, preferably Beaujolais | 2 to 3 tablespoons best-quality balsamic vinegar |
| ½ cup water | |
| 3 tablespoons sugar | |

**1.** Thinly slice 1 cup of the strawberries; set aside. In medium (2-quart) saucepan, combine remaining strawberries, wine, water, and sugar. Bring mixture just to a boil. Reduce heat and simmer, partially covered, 10 minutes. Add cornstarch mixture and stir until thickened, 1 to 2 minutes.

**2.** Transfer mixture to food processor. Puree until smooth. Serve hot or cold, adding vinegar just before serving and garnishing with reserved sliced berries.

### Nutrients Per Serving

| | | | | | |
|---|---|---|---|---|---|
| Calories: | 136 | Cholesterol: | 0 | Vitamin A: | 43 IU |
| Fat: | .6 gm | Sodium: | 5.6 mg | Vitamin C: | 91 gm |
| Sat. fat: | tr | Fiber: | 4 gm | Zinc: | .3 gm |
| Iron: | .8 gm | Cal. from fat: | 4% | | |

Chapter 7

# Vegetable Main Dishes

When you're trying to be prudent about fat intake, the occasional all-vegetable meal is an excellent strategy. It's also a good strategy for building antioxidant nutrients into your diet. That's why we developed a whole set of entrées that revolve around vegetables. If your family loves stuffed cabbage rolls, try our version, which pairs barley-stuffed cabbage with a spectacular red pepper sauce to make a beta-carotene–rich main course that is phenomenally high in vitamin C. And since pasta goes so well with vegetables, four selections pair different pasta shapes with a variety of nutrient-rich vegetables. There's a scrumptious spaghetti made with spinach, ricotta, and basil that is not only rich in antioxidants but contains nearly 500 milligrams of calcium, well more than half the recommended daily dose for this bone-strengthening mineral. Potato-Kale Frittata is also rich in calcium, beta-carotene, and vitamin C. Better yet, it works as an entrée at breakfast, brunch, or a "light"-style dinner.

# Layered Roasted Vegetable Terrine

• This rich terrine is a vegetarian's dream. Meaty eggplant, sublime red peppers, and robust tomatoes are double roasted and layered in a hearty and healthy dish. Try it also as a side dish beside a piece of grilled meat or fish.

Preparation time: 25 minutes, plus 10 minutes resting

Cooking time: 1 hour 15 minutes to 1 hour 20 minutes

Serves 6

| | |
|---|---|
| 1 large eggplant (about 1½ pounds) | ½ cup (packed) Italian (flat-leaf) parsley leaves, chopped |
| Salt | 1 teaspoon grated lemon zest |
| 4 medium zucchini, thinly sliced lengthwise | 4 cloves garlic, minced |
| 4 teaspoons olive oil | 1 teaspoon freshly ground black pepper |
| 6 red bell peppers, roasted (see note, p. 145) | ⅓ cup grated parmesan cheese |
| 1 28-ounce can whole plum tomatoes, roasted (see note, page 107) | |

1.  Preheat broiler.

2.  Slice eggplant ¼ to ½ inch thick. Sprinkle eggplant slices lightly with salt. Place on paper towels and press with a weighted plate for 20 minutes. Rinse and squeeze dry.

3.  Toss eggplant and zucchini slices with the oil. Place on baking sheet and broil until lightly browned, 3 to 4 minutes per side.

4.  Spray an 8½x5½x2½-inch loaf pan with nonstick cooking spray. In small bowl, combine parsley, zest, garlic, pepper, and parmesan. In prepared loaf pan, layer one third of the peppers, half

*continued*

the eggplant, half the tomatoes, half the zucchini, sprinkling the parmesan and herb mixture between each layer. Repeat. Finish with remaining peppers.

5. Cover terrine with foil and bake 40 minutes. Remove foil and cook another 25 minutes. Let rest 10 minutes before cutting.

### Nutrients Per Serving

| Calories: | 240 | Cholesterol: | 5 mg | Vitamin A: | 5,973 IU |
|-----------|-----|--------------|------|------------|----------|
| Fat: | 7.9 gm | Sodium: | 468 mg | Vitamin C: | 277 mg |
| Sat. fat: | .7 gm | Fiber: | 8.4 gm | Zinc: | 1.3 mg |
| Iron: | 6.3 mg | Cal. from fat: | 29% | | |

# Barley-stuffed Cabbage with Red Pepper Sauce

• This antioxidant-rich stuffed cabbage is filled with the flavors of the Middle East. Dried fruit and nuts add not only flavor and texture, but also vitamins.

Preparation time: 30 minutes

Cooking time: 40 minutes

Serves 4

| | |
|---|---|
| 1 head green cabbage, cored and tough leaves removed | 1 cup Italian (flat-leaf) parsley leaves, chopped |
| 2 teaspoons safflower oil | ¼ cup chopped dried apricots |
| 2 cups chopped onion | 2 teaspoons grated orange zest |
| ¼ cup slivered almonds | ½ teaspoon freshly ground black pepper |
| 4 cloves garlic, minced | Salt, to taste (optional) |
| ¼ teaspoon ground allspice | ½ recipe Roasted Red Pepper Sauce (page 121) |
| ¼ teaspoon ground cinnamon | 1 cup vegetable or chicken broth, canned or homemade |
| ¼ teaspoon cayenne pepper | |
| 3 cups cooked barley | |
| 8 ounces plum tomatoes, diced (1½ cups) | |

1. Place cabbage in large (6- to 8-quart) saucepan of boiling water. Simmer until leaves are easily separated, about 10 minutes. Refresh under cold water and drain, inverted. Carefully peel 8 whole leaves off cabbage head; trim outside edge of the leaf until leaf is pliable.

2. Preheat oven to 350°F.

3. In large nonstick skillet, heat oil over medium heat. Add onion and cook until just beginning to brown. Add almonds, garlic, allspice, cinnamon, and cayenne and cook 1 minute more. Stir in barley, tomatoes, parsley, apricots, zest, pepper, salt (if used), and ½ cup Roasted Red Pepper Sauce.

*continued*

**4.** Place one cabbage leaf on work surface. Place ⅓ cup of filling on top. Fold sides in and roll up into small parcel. Place in baking dish. Repeat with remaining filling. Add broth, then cover dish and bake 20 minutes. Serve with Roasted Red Pepper Sauce.

### Nutrients Per Serving

| | | | | | |
|---|---|---|---|---|---|
| Calories: | 376 | Cholesterol: | 0 | Vitamin A: | 4,924 IU |
| Fat: | 9 gm | Sodium: | 315 mg | Vitamin C: | 264 mg |
| Sat. fat: | .9 gm | Fiber: | 7.6 gm | Zinc: | 2.3 mg |
| Iron: | 5.9 mg | Cal. from fat: | 20% | | |

# Potato-Kale Frittata

• This frittata makes for a healthy brunch. It is loaded with flavor, fiber, and nutrients, including iron. Egg substitute keeps the cholesterol content very low.

Preparation time: 15 minutes

Cooking time: 20 to 25 minutes

Serves 4

2 teaspoons olive oil

2 cups thinly sliced onion

3 cups chopped kale (12 ounces)

3 cloves garlic, minced

1 cup diced, cooked potato

1 medium tomato, diced (1 cup)

1½ cups fat-free egg substitute

1 cup grated reduced-fat cheddar cheese (3 ounces)

½ cup tomato paste

¼ cup thin strips ham (optional)

½ teaspoon freshly ground black pepper, or to taste

Salt (optional)

1.   Preheat broiler.

2.   In 10-inch, nonstick ovenproof skillet, heat oil over medium-low heat. Add onion and cook, stirring, until translucent, 7 to 8 minutes. Add kale and garlic and cook until kale is wilted. Tilt pan so oil covers sides. Add potatoes and tomatoes and toss gently.

3.   In small bowl, stir together egg, cheese, tomato paste, ham (if used), pepper, and salt (if used) until well combined.

4.   Add egg mixture to hot skillet and smooth with a spatula. Continue cooking 5 to 6 minutes until egg is almost set, lifting sides of frittata to allow raw egg to run underneath.

5.   Place skillet under broiler to finish cooking, 4 to 5 minutes. Slide frittata out onto plate, cut into wedges, and serve.

*continued*

## Nutrients Per Serving

| | | | | | |
|---|---|---|---|---|---|
| Calories: | 288 | Cholesterol: | 15 mg | Vitamin A: | 9,340 IU |
| Fat: | 7 gm | Sodium: | 620 mg | Vitamin C: | 135 mg |
| Sat. fat: | 3 gm | Fiber: | 9.8 gm | Zinc: | 1.9 mg |
| Iron: | 4.7 mg | Cal. from fat: | 23% | | |

# Carrot and Chickpea Curry

• Enjoy this flavorful curry over rice for an authentic Indian flavor and an incredibly healthy meal. Not only are the carrots, potatoes, and tomatoes chock full of vitamins, but the chickpeas are loaded with fiber.

Preparation time: 20 minutes

Cooking time: 35 minutes

Serves 4

| | |
|---|---|
| 3 cloves garlic, cut up | 1½ cups low-sodium chicken stock, homemade or canned |
| 1 cube (1 inch) ginger, peeled and cut up | 2 cups peeled, cubed (1 inch) potatoes (10 ounces) |
| 3 tablespoons water | |
| 2 tablespoons vegetable oil | 2 cups cooked chickpeas (or 1 16-ounce can, rinsed and drained) |
| ½ cup chopped onion | |
| 1 tablespoon curry powder | 1 large tomato, diced (1½ cups) |
| ½ teaspoon ground cumin | ½ cup (packed) fresh cilantro leaves, chopped |
| ½ teaspoon ground cardamom | |
| ¼ teaspoon ground cinnamon | Salt and freshly ground black pepper, to taste |
| 2 cups peeled mini carrots or 2-inch pieces peeled regular carrots (8 ounces) | |

1.  In food processor, combine garlic, ginger, and water. Puree until smooth.

2.  In large (4-quart) saucepan, heat oil over medium heat. Add onion and cook, stirring, until tender. Add curry powder, cumin, and cinnamon and continue cooking 1 minute.

3.  Add garlic-ginger puree and carrots. Cook 1 minute, stirring. Stir in stock, potatoes, chickpeas, tomatoes, and cilantro; simmer gently, partly covered, about 35 minutes. Season with pepper and salt and serve.

*continued*

## Nutrients Per Serving

| Calories: | 260 | Cholesterol: | 0 | Vitamin A: | 16,456 IU |
|-----------|-----|--------------|---|------------|-----------|
| Fat: | 9.7 gm | Sodium: | 398 mg | Vitamin C: | 35 mg |
| Sat. fat: | 1 gm | Fiber: | 7.7 gm | Zinc: | 1.3 mg |
| Iron: | 3.2 mg | Cal. from fat: | 34% | | |

# Saffron Paella with Artichokes, Tomatoes, and Red Peppers

• Fragrant saffron flavors and colors this Spanish rice dish. Traditionally it is made with chicken and seafood, but this vegetable-based version has become a classic in my kitchen. Strict vegetarians can omit the ham. Try it as a side dish, too.

Preparation time: 25 minutes

Cooking time: 35 to 40 minutes

Serves 4

| | |
|---|---|
| 2½ cups low-sodium chicken or vegetable broth, canned or homemade | 1 can (28 ounces) whole plum tomatoes, drained and coarsely chopped |
| Pinch saffron threads | 1 cup frozen peas, thawed |
| 1 tablespoon olive oil | 4 ounces lean ham (optional), chopped |
| 1 cup chopped onion | 1 tablespoon chopped fresh thyme leaves |
| 2 cloves garlic, minced | 1 10-ounce package frozen artichoke hearts, thawed |
| 2 medium carrots, peeled and sliced (1 cup) | 3 red bell peppers, seeded and cut in 1-inch squares |
| 2 cups medium- or long-grain white rice | |

1. Preheat oven to 350°F.

2. In small (1-quart) saucepan, heat 1 cup of the broth to boiling. Add saffron, remove from heat, and set aside 10 minutes.

3. In paella pan or large skillet, heat oil over medium-high heat. Add onion and garlic and cook, stirring, until translucent, 3 to 4 minutes. Add carrots and rice and stir to coat.

4. Add remaining 1½ cups broth, saffron mixture, and tomatoes; bring to boil; boil 1 minute. Remove from heat. Stir in peas, ham (if used), and thyme and sprinkle top with artichokes and peppers.

continued

**5.** Place in oven. Bake until rice is just tender, 15 to 17 minutes. Remove from oven. Cover and let stand 10 minutes before serving.

| Nutrients Per Serving | | | | | |
|---|---|---|---|---|---|
| Calories: | 500 | Cholesterol: | 2 mg | Vitamin A: | 12,479 IU |
| Fat: | 4 gm | Sodium: | 335 mg | VitaminC: | 157 mg |
| Sat. fat: | .8 gm | Fiber: | 9.5 gm | Zinc: | .84 mg |
| Iron: | 6.3 mg | Cal. from fat: | 7% | | |

# Fusilli with Roasted Vegetables

• Delectable! Roasting vegetables brings out their natural flavors as they melt into a sauce. This recipe is also great with added squash or eggplant. Use your imagination. If you cannot find a yellow pepper, substitute another red one.

Preparation time: 10 minutes

Cooking time: 45 minutes

Serves 4

| | |
|---|---|
| 1 large red onion, halved and then sliced | 1 tablespoon chopped fresh thyme leaves |
| 2 red bell peppers, seeded and cut in ½-inch strips | ½ teaspoon freshly ground black pepper |
| 2 yellow bell peppers, seeded and cut in ½-inch strips | 1½ tablespoons olive oil |
| 2 green bell peppers, seeded and cut in ½-inch strips | 10 ounces spiral pasta |
| 4 fresh plum tomatoes, cut in thin wedges | ¼ cup (packed) fresh basil leaves, finely shredded |
| 3 cloves garlic, quartered | 1 tablespoon grated parmesan cheese |

**1.** Preheat oven to 400°F.

**2.** In one large roasting pan combine onions, all bell peppers, tomatoes, garlic, thyme, black pepper, and olive oil. Place in oven and roast for 40 minutes, tossing and mixing vegetables after 20 minutes.

**3.** Meanwhile, cook pasta according to package directions. Drain, reserving ½ cup cooking liquid.

4. Toss pasta with vegetables, reserved cooking liquid, basil, and parmesan.

*continued*

## Nutrients Per Serving

| | | | | | |
|---|---|---|---|---|---|
| Calories: | 365 | Cholesterol: | 1 mg | Vitamin A: | 1,424 IU |
| Fat: | 6.8 gm | Sodium: | 39 mg | Vitamin C: | 76 mg |
| Sat. fat: | 1 gm | Fiber: | 3.7 gm | Zinc: | 1 mg |
| Iron: | 4 mg | Cal. from fat: | 17% | | |

# Orecchiete with Wilted Greens and Roasted Tomatoes

- Any bitter greens can be used in this recipe. Try kale or chard, or dandelion, mustard, or beet greens. They are all loaded with vitamin A.

Preparation time: 10 minutes

Cooking time: 8 to 10 minutes, plus pasta cooking time

Serves 4

| | |
|---|---|
| 10 ounces orecchiete or small pasta shells | 1 tablespoon red wine vinegar |
| 1 tablespoon olive oil | 1 can (28 ounces) whole plum tomatoes, drained, roasted (see note), and quartered |
| 2 cloves garlic, crushed with flat side of knife | 1 teaspoon freshly ground black pepper |
| 1 pound greens, washed well, thick stalks removed, leaves torn in 2-inch pieces (4 cups, packed) | |

1. Cook pasta according to package directions. Drain, reserving ¼ cup cooking liquid.

2. In large nonstick skillet, heat oil over medium heat. Add garlic and cook until slightly golden, 1 to 2 minutes. Add greens, raise heat to high, and cook, tossing constantly, until just wilted, 4 to 5 minutes. Add pasta, reserved cooking liquid, and pepper. Toss well. Serve promptly.

### Note

To roast tomatoes, preheat oven to 350°F. Drain whole canned tomatoes; place on lightly oiled baking sheet. Roast 90 minutes, turning after 45, until very soft and slightly blackened. (One 28-ounce can will yield about 14 tomatoes.)

*continued*

### Nutrients Per Serving

| | | | | | |
|---|---|---|---|---|---|
| Calories: | 371 | Cholesterol: | 0 | Vitamin A: | 7,361 IU |
| Fat: | 5.4 gm | Sodium: | 358 mg | Vitamin C: | 113 mg |
| Sat. fat: | .7 gm | Fiber: | 8 gm | Zinc: | 1.5 mg |
| Iron: | 5.2 mg | Cal. from fat: | 13% | | |

# Penne with Double-Tomato Herb Sauce

- This sauce is bright, light, and flavorful, as well as a great iron source for nonmeat-eaters. Penne is a tubular pasta shape. *Rigate* means "ridged." Look for penne with these ridges on the outside. It is readily available.

Preparation time: 10 minutes

Cooking time: 20 to 25 minutes

Serves 4

| | |
|---|---|
| ⅓ cup chopped sun-dried tomatoes (1½ ounces) | 1½ teaspoons grated orange zest |
| 1 cup boiling water | 1 bay leaf |
| 1 tablespoon extra virgin olive oil | 10 ounces penne rigate |
| 1 cup chopped onion | ⅓ cup (packed) fresh basil leaves, chopped |
| 3 cloves garlic, minced | 1 teaspoon chopped fresh thyme leaves |
| 1 can (28 ounces) whole plum tomatoes in juice | |

1. Combine sun-dried tomatoes and boiling water. Set aside for 10 minutes.

2. In large nonstick skillet, heat oil over medium heat. Add onion and cook until translucent, 4 to 5 minutes. Add garlic and cook 1 minute more.

3. Stir in sun-dried tomatoes along with water, plum tomatoes and juice, zest, and bay leaf. Bring mixture to boil. Reduce heat to low and simmer, breaking up tomatoes with back of wooden spoon, until thickened, about 15 minutes.

4. Meanwhile cook pasta according to package directions. Drain, reserving ½ cup cooking liquid.

*continued*

**5.** In large bowl, combine pasta, sauce (first removing bay leaf), reserved cooking liquid, and herbs. Toss well.

### Nutrients Per Serving

| | | | | | |
|---|---|---|---|---|---|
| Calories: | 391 | Cholesterol: | 0 | Vitamin A: | 3,403 IU |
| Fat: | 5.6 gm | Sodium: | 345 mg | Vitamin C: | 67 mg |
| Sat. fat: | .8 gm | Fiber: | 6.3 gm | Zinc: | 1.5 mg |
| Iron: | 5.7 mg | Cal. from fat: | 13% | | |

# Spaghetti with Spinach Ricotta and Basil

• The sauce on this dish tastes like a creamy pesto without all of the fat from oil and nuts. It does have lots of spinach and ricotta, however, which makes it a rich source of calcium as well as of beta-carotene and iron.

Preparation time: 10 minutes

Cooking time: 10 minutes

Serves 4

| | |
|---|---|
| 2 packages (10-ounces each) frozen chopped spinach | 1½ teaspoons freshly ground black pepper |
| 1 cup part-skim ricotta | 12 ounces spaghetti |
| ½ cup (packed) fresh basil leaves | |
| ¼ cup freshly grated parmesan cheese | |

**1.** Cook spinach according to package directions. Drain well. In food processor, combine spinach, ricotta, basil, parmesan, and pepper; puree until smooth.

**2.** Meanwhile, cook pasta according to package directions. Drain, reserving ½ cup cooking liquid.

**3.** In large bowl, combine pasta, spinach mixture, and reserved cooking liquid. Toss well.

### Nutrients Per Serving

| Calories: | 420 | Cholesterol: | 24 mg | Vitamin A: | 11,623 IU |
|---|---|---|---|---|---|
| Fat: | 8 gm | Sodium: | 302 mg | Vitamin C: | 37 mg |
| Sat. fat: | 4.4 gm | Fiber: | 4.8 gm | Zinc: | 2.7 mg |
| Iron: | 7.6 mg | Cal. from fat: | 18% | | |

# Red and Green Pepper Lasagne

- The richness in this classic dish does not come from meat. Rather, it comes from sautéed peppers packed with antioxidants and bursting with flavor.

Preparation time: 40 minutes

Cooking time: 60 minutes

Serves 6–8

| | |
|---|---|
| 8 ounces lasagna noodles (9 sheets) | 1 cup low-fat (1%) cottage cheese |
| 1 tablespoon safflower oil | 2 large eggs, lightly beaten |
| 2 medium onions, thinly sliced | ½ teaspoon freshly ground black pepper |
| 4 red bell peppers, seeded and cut in ⅛-inch strips | ¼ cup (packed) fresh basil leaves, chopped |
| 4 green bell peppers, seeded and cut in ⅛-inch strips | 2 tablespoons grated parmesan cheese |
| Salt, to taste (optional) | 2½ cups tomato sauce, homemade or store-bought |
| Freshly ground black pepper, to taste | |
| 1 cup part-skim ricotta cheese | 1 cup shredded part-skim or nonfat mozzarella |

1. Preheat oven to 400°F.

2. Cook lasagna noodles in plenty of water, until just tender. Drain and place them in cold water until needed.

3. While pasta is cooking, heat oil in large nonstick skillet over medium heat. Add onions and cook, stirring, until wilted. Add bell peppers and cook until tender, about 15 minutes. Cover and continue cooking 10 minutes. Season with salt (if used) and pepper to taste.

**4.** In medium bowl, combine ricotta, cottage cheese, eggs, black pepper, basil, and parmesan.

**5.** In a 12×9×2-inch lasagne pan or baking dish, spread ½ cup tomato sauce, then layer of 3 noodles, ½ cup sauce, half ricotta mixture, half vegetable mixture, and ⅓ cup mozzarella; repeat, ending with final layer of 3 noodles. Spread top noodles with remaining 1 cup sauce and sprinkle with remaining cheese.

**6.** Bake until cheese is melted and sauce is bubbly, about 60 minutes. Allow lasagne to sit for 10 minutes before cutting.

| Nutrients Per Serving | | | | | |
|---|---|---|---|---|---|
| Calories: | 345 | Cholesterol: | 72 mg | Vitamin A: | 3,916 IU |
| Fat: | 10 gm | Sodium: | 825 mg | Vitamin C: | 133 mg |
| Sat. fat: | 4.1 gm | Fiber: | 4.2 gm | Zinc: | 2 mg |
| Iron: | 3.1 mg | Cal. from fat: | 26% | | |

# Carrot and Broccoli Risotto

• Risotto can be served either as a main course or as an appetizer. In this version, creamy arborio rice is enhanced with vitamin-rich carrot and broccoli. Because it is very filling, serve a half portion to begin a meal. Either way, you will get plenty of beta-carotene and iron.

Serve with additional grated parmesan on the side.

Preparation time: 5 minutes

Cooking time: 30 to 35 minutes

Serves 4 or 8 as an appetizer

| | |
|---|---|
| 5 cups low-sodium chicken or vegetable broth, canned or homemade | 2 cups ½-inch broccoli florets |
| 1 tablespoon olive oil | 2 carrots, peeled and grated (1 cup) |
| 2 carrots, peeled and finely diced (1 cup) | 2 tablespoons grated parmesan cheese, plus additional for serving |
| ½ cup chopped shallots | 1 tablespoon fresh lemon juice |
| 1 cup finely diced fennel | 2 teaspoons grated lemon zest |
| 2 cups arborio or any medium-grain rice | 2 teaspoons chopped fresh thyme leaves |
| ¼ cup dry white wine | ½ teaspoon salt, or more to taste |
| | Freshly ground pepper, to taste |

1.  Bring chicken or vegetable broth to boiling. Lower heat to simmer.

2.  In wide, heavy-bottomed large (4½-quart) saucepan, heat oil over medium heat. Add diced carrots and shallots and cook until shallots begin to soften, about 6 minutes. Add fennel and rice and cook, stirring constantly, until rice is well coated, 1 to 2 minutes. Add wine and cook until absorbed.

**3.** Add 1 cup simmering broth and continue cooking, stirring until the stock is almost all absorbed. Continue adding broth, ½ cup at a time, stirring and cooking until broth is absorbed and rice comes away from side of pot before each addition. Continue until all but 1½ cups of the broth has been absorbed, 15 to 20 minutes.

**4.** Add broccoli and grated carrots and continue cooking and adding the broth, ¼ cup at a time, until rice is creamy yet kernels are firm in center. This should take another 5 to 10 minutes.

**5.** Remove from heat, stir in parmesan, juice, zest, thyme, salt, and pepper. Serve immediately.

| Nutrients Per Main-Dish Serving | | | | | |
|---|---|---|---|---|---|
| Calories: | 478 | Cholesterol: | 2 mg | Vitamin A: | 8,469 IU |
| Fat: | 6.5 gm | Sodium: | 447 mg | Vitamin C: | 50 mg |
| Sat. fat: | 1 gm | Fiber: | 3.9 gm | Zinc: | 1.4 mg |
| Iron: | 5.5 mg | Cal. from fat: | 12% | | |

## Chapter 8

# Meat, Fish, and Poultry Main Dishes

Look to this category as your main source for zinc, the mineral that seems crucial to a healthy immune system. Elegant fish main dishes like the Grilled Swordfish with Mango Salsa, the Oven-steamed Salmon with Roasted Pepper and Onion Compote, the Fish Cooked in Spicy Tomato Sauce, and the Linguine with Clams, Red Peppers, and Broccoli are also notable sources of the antioxidant mineral selenium. Shepherd's Pie with Sweet Potato Topping, an excellent source of beta-carotene, also contains a small amount of vitamin E. So does the Veal, Spinach, and Provençal Herb Lasagne.

# Braised Chicken with Apricots and Ginger

• Dried apricots, a good source of vitamin A and fiber, are cooked with chicken in this savory braised dish. This Moroccan-inspired entrée is fragrant, sweet and spicy, and oh so healthy.

Preparation time: 8 minutes

Cooking time: 90 minutes

Serves 4

| | |
|---|---|
| 8 small chicken thighs, skin and excess fat removed | 1 2x1-inch piece orange zest |
| 1 teaspoon freshly ground black pepper | 2 teaspoons ground cardamom |
| ½ teaspoon salt | 1 teaspoon ground turmeric |
| 2 teaspoons safflower oil | ¾ teaspoon ground cloves |
| 1½ cups chopped onion | 1 cup low-sodium chicken broth, canned or homemade, or water |
| 1 tablespoon grated fresh ginger | 1 cup dried apricots (6 ounces), sliced in ⅛- to ¼-inch strips |
| 2 cloves garlic, minced | |

1. Preheat oven to 350°F. Sprinkle chicken pieces with pepper and salt.

2. In Dutch oven, heat oil over medium heat. Add onion and cook until translucent. Add ginger, garlic, orange zest, cardamom, turmeric, and cloves and continue cooking 1 minute. Add stock or water and apricots. Remove from heat.

3. Nestle chicken pieces in apricot mixture. Cover pot with foil, then with lid to create air-tight seal. Place in oven and cook until chicken is tender, about 90 minutes.

*continued*

## Nutrients Per Serving

| | | | | | |
|---|---|---|---|---|---|
| Calories: | 260 | Cholesterol: | 86 mg | Vitamin A: | 2,425 IU |
| Fat: | 7 gm | Sodium: | 529 mg | Vitamin C: | 9 mg |
| Sat. fat: | 1.3 gm | Fiber: | 3.6 gm | Zinc: | 2.4 mg |
| Iron: | 3.3 mg | Cal. from fat: | 24% | | |

# Broiled Chicken with Roasted Pepper Sauce

- Once you make this vitamin A- and C-rich roasted pepper sauce, you will want to serve it on everything. There is no reason not to. It is spectacular with beef, fish, or even pasta.

Preparation time: 10 minutes

Cooking time: 10 minutes

Serves 4

| | |
|---|---|
| 4 chicken pieces, skin and excess fat removed | 8 red bell peppers, roasted (see note page 145) |
| 1 tablespoon chopped fresh rosemary leaves | 1 clove garlic, crushed through a press |
| 1 teaspoon freshly ground black pepper | 1 tablespoon fresh lemon juice |
| ½ teaspoon salt (optional) | 1 teaspoon safflower oil |

**1.** Preheat broiler.

**2.** Sprinkle chicken pieces with rosemary, pepper, and salt. Broil, 4 inches from heat, until cooked through, about 10 minutes, turning once.

**3.** Meanwhile, in food processor, combine roasted peppers, garlic, juice, and oil. Puree until smooth.

**4.** Pool sauce on serving plates. Place chicken on top.

### Nutrients Per Serving

| | | | | | |
|---|---|---|---|---|---|
| Calories: | 238 | Cholesterol: | 68 mg | Vitamin A: | 5,597 IU |
| Fat: | .5 gm | Sodium: | 81 mg | Vitamin C: | 256 mg |
| Sat. fat: | .5 gm | Fiber: | 2.8 gm | Zinc: | 1 mg |
| Iron: | 1.7 mg | Cal. from fat: | 2% | | |

# Grilled Swordfish with Mango Salsa

• This is my favorite way of preparing fish in the summer. Selenium-rich swordfish is perfect for an outdoor grill, either as a steak or on skewers with cherry tomatoes. The refreshing salsa is an ideal accompaniment.

Preparation time: 20 minutes

Cooking time: 8 to 12 minutes

Serves 4

| | |
|---|---|
| 4 swordfish steaks (6 ounces each) | ⅓ cup (packed) fresh cilantro leaves, chopped |
| ½ cup plus 3 tablespoons fresh lime juice | 1 tablespoon grated fresh ginger |
| 1 tablespoon extra virgin olive oil | ½ teaspoon freshly ground black pepper |
| 2 mangoes, peeled, seeded, and diced (2 cups) | ¼ teaspoon grated lime zest |
| 2 medium tomatoes, peeled, seeded, and diced (2 cups) | Salt, to taste (optional) |
| ½ cup diced red onion | |

**1.**   Preheat grill or broiler.

**2.**   Place fish in shallow dish. In small bowl, combine ½ cup lime juice and oil; pour over fish. Cover fish with plastic wrap and set aside 20 minutes.

**3.**   To make salsa: In medium bowl, combine mangoes, tomatoes, onion, cilantro, 3 tablespoons lime juice, ginger, pepper, zest, and salt (if used). Set aside for 10 minutes.

**4.**   Grill or broil swordfish, 4 to 5 inches from heat, until just cooked through, 8 to 12 minutes. Serve with salsa.

| Calories: | 287 | Cholesterol: | 59 mg | Vitamin A: | 4,004 IU |
|-----------|-----|--------------|-------|-----------|----------|
| Fat: | 8 gm | Sodium: | 153 mg | Vitamin C: | 46 mg |
| Sat. fat: | 2 gm | Fiber: | 2.4 gm | Zinc: | 1.8 mg |
| Iron: | 2 mg | Cal. from fat: | 26% | | |

# Oven-steamed Salmon with Roasted Pepper and Onion Compote

• Onions, peppers, and herbs melt into a rich compote on which the fish is cooked. This recipe is a good reason to keep roasted peppers on hand. Stored in their own juices, they will keep for up to a week in the refrigerator.

Preparation time: 20 minutes

Cooking time: 18 to 20 minutes

Serves 4

| | |
|---|---|
| 2 cups very thinly sliced red onion | 4 salmon fillets (5 ounces each) |
| 4 peppers, preferably a mixture of different types, roasted (see note page 145) | ½ cup dry white wine |
| | 3 tablespoons fresh lemon juice |
| 4 cloves garlic, minced | ½ teaspoon freshly ground black pepper |
| 2 tablespoons chopped fresh thyme leaves | |

**1.**   Preheat oven to 450°F.

**2.**   In a 13x9x2-inch baking dish, combine onion, peppers (and any pepper juice), garlic, and thyme. Top with salmon, then add wine, lemon juice, and pepper. Cover tightly with foil poked with a few small holes.

**3.**   Place dish in oven and bake until fish is cooked through, 18 to 20 minutes. Serve by placing vegetables on individual plates and topping each portion with salmon.

| Calories: | 284 | Cholesterol: | 78 mg | Vitamin A: | 2,897 IU |
|---|---|---|---|---|---|
| Fat: | 9.3 gm | Sodium: | 77 mg | Vitamin C: | 139 mg |
| Sat. fat: | 1.4 gm | Fiber: | 2.7 gm | Zinc: | .2 mg |
| Iron: | 2.8 mg | Cal. from fat: | 29% | | |

# Fish Cooked in Spicy Tomato Sauce

• Use this quick, tasty tomato sauce, enhanced with the spicy flavors of southern France, to cook any type of fish or shellfish. This low-fat dish is great made with fresh summer tomatoes.

Preparation time: 10 minutes

Cooking time: 25 to 30 minutes

Serves 4

| | |
|---|---|
| 2 teaspoons olive oil | 1 cup water |
| 1 cup chopped onion | 1 teaspoon grated orange zest |
| 2 cloves garlic, minced | ¼ to ½ teaspoon hot pepper flakes |
| ¾ cup dry white wine | 1 sprig fresh rosemary |
| 1 can (28 ounces) whole plum tomatoes in juice, coarsely chopped | 4 cod fillets (6 ounces each) |

**1.** In large nonstick skillet, heat oil over medium-high heat. Add onion and cook, stirring, until tender, 4 to 5 minutes. Add garlic and cook 1 minute. Add wine and continue cooking, stirring until evaporated.

**2.** Add tomatoes and juice, water, zest, pepper flakes, and whole rosemary sprig. Simmer until thickened, 15 minutes.

**3.** Nestle fish fillets in tomato sauce. Partially cover and cook until fish is just cooked through, 4 to 8 minutes, depending on thickness. Serve fillets topped with sauce, first removing rosemary sprig.

| Calories: | 220 | Cholesterol: | 73 mg | Vitamin A: | 1,345 IU |
|-----------|-----|--------------|-------|-----------|----------|
| Fat: | 4 gm | Sodium: | 419 mg | Vitamin C: | 36 mg |
| Sat. fat: | 6 gm | Fiber: | 2.2 gm | Zinc: | 1.2 mg |
| Iron: | 2.2 mg | Cal. from fat: | 16% | | |

# Beefsteak with Tomato-Orange Salsa

• The piquant salsa here is ideal with beef, but try it on grilled fish for a healthy taste of the Mediterranean.

Preparation time: 15 minutes, plus marinating time

Cooking time: 10 to 20 minutes

Serves 4

2 medium tomatoes, diced (2 cups)

1 cup thinly sliced red onion

1 cup orange sections (see note page 201)

4 teaspoons extra virgin olive oil

16 black olives, pitted and slivered

1 teaspoon chopped fresh thyme leaves

¼ teaspoon cayenne pepper

Salt, to taste (optional)

4 beefsteak, such as London broil (top round) (4 to 5 ounces)

**1.** In medium bowl, combine tomatoes, onion, orange sections, olive oil, olives, thyme, cayenne pepper, and salt (if used). Cover and set salsa aside for 30 minutes.

**2.** Broil steak, 4 inches from heat, to desired doneness, 10 to 20 minutes. Serve topped with salsa.

### Nutrients Per Serving

| | | | | | |
|---|---|---|---|---|---|
| Calories: | 267 | Cholesterol: | 80 mg | Vitamin A: | 780 IU |
| Fat: | 9 gm | Sodium: | 203 mg | Vitamin C: | 45 mg |
| Sat. fat: | 2.2 gm | Fiber: | 3.3 gm | Zinc: | 5.5 mg |
| Iron: | 4 mg | Cal. from fat: | 30% | | |

# Tomato-stuffed Pork Tenderloin with Roasted Poblano Sauce

- If you choose to use canned tomatoes, try an organic brand. They really burst with fresh flavor. You may substitute any type of peppers for the poblanos.

Preparation time: 20 minutes

Cooking time: 18 to 20 minutes

Serves 4

| | |
|---|---|
| 4 poblano peppers, roasted (see note page 145) | 2 pork tenderloins (8 ounces each) |
| ¼ cup water | 2 cloves garlic, minced |
| 1 tablespoon fresh lemon juice | ¼ teaspoon salt |
| 3 teaspoons extra virgin olive oil | 1 tablespoon chopped fresh thyme leaves |
| Salt, to taste | 14 tomatoes, canned or fresh, roasted (see note page 107) |

1. Preheat grill or broiler.

2. In food processor, combine peppers, water, lemon juice, 2 teaspoons of the oil, and salt to taste. Puree until smooth. Set aside.

3. Slice tenderloins lengthwise almost all the way through; open on work surface. Pound tenderloins gently, without breaking through meat, until ⅛ to ¼ inch thick. Rub each with remaining ½ teaspoon olive oil.

4. Chop garlic with ¼ teaspoon salt, pressing it into smooth paste with side of knife. Spread on tenderloins and sprinkle with thyme. Line 7 tomatoes along long edge of each tenderloin. Roll up tenderloin tightly, securing ends and middle with toothpicks.

*continued*

**5.** Grill or broil pork, turning gradually, until browned on all sides and cooked through, 18 to 20 minutes. Remove from heat, remove toothpicks, and let rest 5 minutes. Cut, against the grain, into ¾-inch slices and serve with poblano sauce.

### Nutrients Per Serving

| | | | | | |
|---|---|---|---|---|---|
| Calories: | 260 | Cholesterol: | 71 mg | Vitamin A: | 1,870 IU |
| Fat: | 10.3 gm | Sodium: | 514 mg | Vitamin C: | 238 mg |
| Sat. fat: | 2.8 gm | Fiber: | 2.5 gm | Zinc: | 2.8 mg |
| Iron: | 3.6 mg | Cal. from fat: | 36% | | |

# Moroccan Lamb and Vegetable Stew

• The sweet and aromatic flavors of northern Africa make this lamb stew an exquisite meal, rich in antioxidants and other nutrients. Serve it with couscous for a traditional touch.

Preparation time: 20 minutes

Cooking time: 1 hour 50 minutes to 2 hours 10 minutes

Serves 4

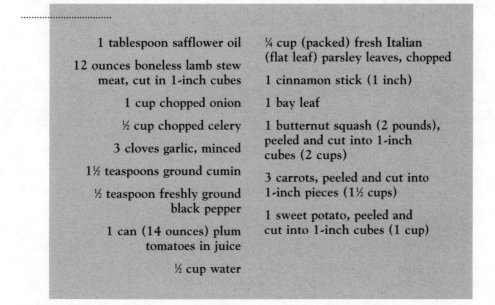

1 tablespoon safflower oil

12 ounces boneless lamb stew meat, cut in 1-inch cubes

1 cup chopped onion

½ cup chopped celery

3 cloves garlic, minced

1½ teaspoons ground cumin

½ teaspoon freshly ground black pepper

1 can (14 ounces) plum tomatoes in juice

½ cup water

¼ cup (packed) fresh Italian (flat leaf) parsley leaves, chopped

1 cinnamon stick (1 inch)

1 bay leaf

1 butternut squash (2 pounds), peeled and cut into 1-inch cubes (2 cups)

3 carrots, peeled and cut into 1-inch pieces (1½ cups)

1 sweet potato, peeled and cut into 1-inch cubes (1 cup)

1. Preheat oven to 350°F.

2. In Dutch oven, heat oil over medium-high heat. Add lamb and brown on all sides, 3 to 4 minutes. With slotted spoon, remove lamb from pan. Set aside.

3. Reduce heat to medium, add onion and celery, and cook, covered, until wilted, 5 to 6 minutes. Add garlic, cumin, and pepper and cook for another minute, stirring.

*continued*

**4.** Add tomatoes and juice, water, parsley, cinnamon stick, and bay leaf. Return lamb and juices to the pan. Bring mixture just to boil, then tightly cover Dutch oven with foil and lid, and place in oven. Bake about 1 hour. Add squash, carrots, and sweet potato. Return to oven and continue cooking until meat is tender, 40 to 60 minutes. Remove cinnamon stick and bay leaf before serving.

### Nutrients Per Serving

| Calories: | 270 | Cholesterol: | 54 mg | Vitamin A: | 24,577 IU |
|---|---|---|---|---|---|
| Fat: | 8 gm | Sodium: | 254 mg | Vitamin C: | 49 mg |
| Sat. fat: | 1.7 gm | Fiber: | 4.2 gm | Zinc: | 3.8 mg |
| Iron: | 4 mg | Cal. from fat: | 26% | | |

# Shepherd's Pie with Sweet Potato Topping

- Here is a version of shepherd's pie with a couple of surprising ingredients—spinach, sweet potatoes, and tomatoes. The result is a beautifully colored and healthy version of a home-style classic.

Preparation time: 10 minutes

Cooking time: 1 hour 40 minutes to 2 hours

Serves 4

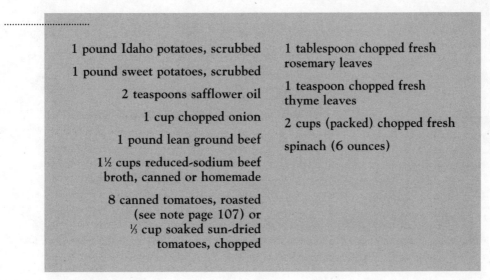

1 pound Idaho potatoes, scrubbed

1 pound sweet potatoes, scrubbed

2 teaspoons safflower oil

1 cup chopped onion

1 pound lean ground beef

1½ cups reduced-sodium beef broth, canned or homemade

8 canned tomatoes, roasted (see note page 107) or ⅓ cup soaked sun-dried tomatoes, chopped

1 tablespoon chopped fresh rosemary leaves

1 teaspoon chopped fresh thyme leaves

2 cups (packed) chopped fresh spinach (6 ounces)

1. Preheat oven to 400°F.

2. Bake Idaho and sweet potatoes until soft, 45 to 60 minutes. Remove from oven, reducing oven temperature to 375°F. When potatoes are cool enough to handle, peel. In large bowl, combine potatoes and mash with a potato masher. Set aside.

3. In large nonstick skillet, heat oil over medium-high heat. Add onion and cook, stirring until it begins to brown, 5 to 6 minutes. Reduce heat to medium. Add beef and continue

*continued*

cooking, stirring, until beef is no longer pink. Add broth, tomatoes, rosemary, and thyme. Simmer 10 minutes.

4.   Add spinach and cook, stirring, until spinach is just wilted. Remove from heat.

5.   Transfer mixture to a 6-cup baking dish and spoon mashed potatoes over the top of the mixture, covering it completely. Bake until top is golden, about 45 minutes.

### Nutrients Per Serving

| Calories: | 411 | Cholesterol: | 70 mg | Vitamin A: | 19,946 IU |
|-----------|-----|--------------|-------|-----------|-----------|
| Fat: | 12.4 gm | Sodium: | 552 mg | Vitamin C: | 67 mg |
| Sat. fat: | 4.5 gm | Fiber: | 6.5 gm | Zinc: | 6 mg |
| Iron: | 5.6 mg | Cal. from fat: | 27% | | |

# Veal, Spinach, and Provençal Herb Lasagne

•   Here is a totally new version of lasagne, without tomato sauce but packed with spinach, so there's lots of iron and antioxidant nutrients. The veal is rich with fragrant herbs and the deep flavors of French country cooking.

Preparation time: 40 minutes

Cooking time: 1 hour 20 minutes

Serves 8

| | |
|---|---|
| 1½ cups low-fat (1%) milk | 3 tablespoons chopped fresh sage leaves |
| 3 cups beef broth, canned or homemade | 1 tablespoon chopped fresh rosemary leaves |
| 4 teaspoons safflower oil | 2 teaspoons grated lemon zest |
| 3 tablespoons unbleached all-purpose flour | ¼ teaspoon grated nutmeg |
| 2 teaspoons extra virgin olive oil | 2 pounds spinach leaves (12 cups, packed), well washed and torn into 2-inch pieces |
| 2 cups chopped onion | |
| 2 carrots, peeled and finely diced (1 cup) | 8 ounces lasagna noodles (9 sheets) |
| 1 pound lean ground veal | |
| ½ cup (packed) Italian (flat leaf) parsley leaves, chopped | |

1.   In small (1-quart) saucepan, heat milk and 1½ cups broth to just simmering. In medium (2-quart) saucepan, heat safflower oil over medium-low heat. Add flour and cook, stirring constantly with whisk, until mixture is thick and golden, about 3 minutes. Slowly add the milk and broth, whisking constantly. Stir out any lumps that form. Continue cooking and whisking, over low heat, until thick, about 10 minutes.

2.   In large nonstick skillet, heat olive oil over medium heat. Add onion and carrots and cook,

*continued*

stirring, until onion is browned, 7 to 8 minutes. Add veal and cook, stirring, until it is no longer pink.

**3.** Add remaining 1½ cups broth, herbs, zest, and nutmeg to meat mixture. Cover and simmer until meat is tender, 30 minutes.

**4.** Meanwhile, steam spinach leaves until just wilted. Chop coarsely, squeeze slightly, and set aside. Cook lasagna noodles in plenty of water, until just tender. Drain and place them in cold water until needed.

**5.** Preheat oven to 350°F.

**6.** In a 13×9×2-inch lasagna pan or baking dish, spread ½ cup meat sauce, then layer of 3 noodles, half the spinach, half the remaining meat sauce, and ¾ cup white sauce. Add another layer of 3 noodles, remaining spinach, remaining meat sauce, and ¾ cup white sauce. Cover with layer of remaining noodles. Spread the top with remaining white sauce.

**7.** Bake until sauce is bubbly, about 30 minutes. Allow lasagne to sit for 10 minutes before cutting.

| Nutrients Per Serving | | | | | |
|---|---|---|---|---|---|
| Calories: | 302 | Cholesterol: | 48 mg | Vitamin A: | 11,792 IU |
| Fat: | 8.7 gm | Sodium: | 404 mg | Vitamin C: | 40 mg |
| Sat. fat: | 2.4 gm | Fiber: | 4.9 gm | Zinc: | 3 mg |
| Iron: | 5 mg | Cal. from fat: | 26% | | |

# Fettuccine with Chicken, Tomatoes, and Basil

• If you are a tomato lover, you will surely be a fan of this dish. Fresh tomatoes are just warmed through to create a simple but perfect pasta sauce. For a vegetarian entrée, just leave out the cooked chicken.

Preparation time: 15 minutes

Cooking time: 2 minutes

Serves 4

| | |
|---|---|
| 10 ounces fettuccine | 1 cup (packed) fresh basil leaves, slivered |
| 1 tablespoon olive oil | ¼ teaspoon freshly ground black pepper |
| 2 cloves garlic, minced | Salt, to taste |
| 1½ pounds ripe tomatoes, cut in 1-inch pieces | |
| 2 cups shredded, cooked chicken breast | |

1. Cook pasta according to package directions. Drain, reserving ⅓ cup cooking liquid.

2. In large nonstick skillet, heat oil over medium heat. Add garlic and cook 1 minute. Add tomatoes and reserved cooking liquid. Increase heat to high and cook, just enough to warm through, about 1 minute. Add pasta and chicken and toss to coat.

3. Remove from heat. Add basil, pepper, and salt, and serve promptly.

### Nutrients Per Serving

| | | | | | |
|---|---|---|---|---|---|
| Calories: | 483 | Cholesterol: | 130 mg | Vitamin A: | 1,564 IU |
| Fat: | 12.3 gm | Sodium: | 92 mg | Vitamin C: | 35 mg |
| Sat. fat: | 2.6 gm | Fiber: | 4.2 gm | Zinc: | 3 mg |
| Iron: | 6.8 mg | Cal. from fat: | 23% | | |

# Linguine with Clams, Broccoli, and Peppers

• Here we have an iron-rich version of a classic Italian dish. The colors of the Italian flag are there, and so is lots of vitamin C.

Preparation time: 15 minutes

Cooking time: 15 minutes

Serves 4

2 dozen clams, washed well

½ cup water

12 ounces linguine

1 tablespoon olive oil

½ cup chopped onion

¾ cup finely shredded red bell pepper

⅓ cup dry white wine

2 cups broccoli florets, steamed to crisp-tender

¼ cup (packed) fresh basil leaves, chopped

Salt, to taste (optional)

Freshly ground black pepper, to taste

**1.** Place clams and water in large pot, over high heat. Cover and steam until clams open, 3 to 5 minutes. Carefully pour liquid into a bowl, discarding any unopened shells and sand. Remove clams from shells, chop, and place in the liquid. Reserve.

**2.** Meanwhile, cook linguine according to package directions. Drain well.

**3.** In large nonstick skillet, heat oil over medium heat. Add onion and red pepper and cook until onion is translucent. Add the clam liquid and wine and continue cooking 3 minutes.

**4.** Add cooked linguine to the skillet and toss with sauce, clams, broccoli, and basil. Season with salt (if used) and pepper.

| Calories: | 460 | Cholesterol: | 31 mg | Vitamin A: | 2,471 IU |
|---|---|---|---|---|---|
| Fat: | 5.8 gm | Sodium: | 74 mg | Vitamin C: | 84 mg |
| Sat. fat: | .7 gm | Fiber: | 4.9 gm | Zinc: | 2.4 mg |
| Iron: | 17 mg | Cal. from fat: | 17% | | |

## Chapter 9

# Main-Dish Salads

Like the main-dish meat, fish, and poultry recipes, these salads often contain small amounts of zinc and iron (due to their meat content). Salads that contain seafood, like the flavorful Italian Seafood Salad and the Thai-inspired Mango and Fennel Salad with Shrimp and Peanuts, also deliver small amounts of selenium. Each of these salad presentations, due to the colorful addition of beta-carotene- and vitamin C–rich fruits, looks spectacular and tastes far more exciting than traditional salad bar fare. They can be particularly welcome additions to your antioxidant-rich diet during the hot summer months, when raw and chilled vegetables are more enticing than the cooked variety.

# Sliced Steak and Roasted Tomato Salad

• The deep flavors of roasted tomatoes, beef, and arugula make this salad a hearty and pungent meal—and one that is rich in vitamins A and C.

Preparation time: 10 minutes, plus 5 minutes resting time

Cooking time: approximately 10 minutes

Serves 4

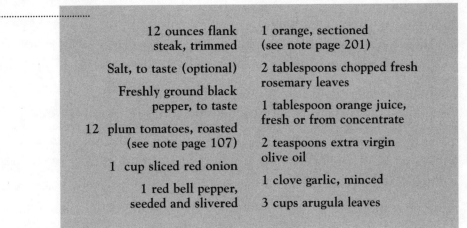

| | |
|---|---|
| 12 ounces flank steak, trimmed | 1 orange, sectioned (see note page 201) |
| Salt, to taste (optional) | 2 tablespoons chopped fresh rosemary leaves |
| Freshly ground black pepper, to taste | 1 tablespoon orange juice, fresh or from concentrate |
| 12 plum tomatoes, roasted (see note page 107) | 2 teaspoons extra virgin olive oil |
| 1 cup sliced red onion | 1 clove garlic, minced |
| 1 red bell pepper, seeded and slivered | 3 cups arugula leaves |

**1.** Preheat broiler.

**2.** Season steak with salt (if used) and black pepper to taste. Broil, 4-6 inches from heat, to desired doneness. Allow meat to rest 5 minutes. Slice thinly against the grain.

**3.** In large bowl, combine tomatoes, onion, red pepper, orange, rosemary, orange juice, olive oil, garlic, ½ teaspoon black pepper, and salt (if used). Toss gently until combined.

**4.** Add arugula to mixture. Toss gently. Arrange on plates along with steak. Serve promptly.

*continued*

### Nutrients Per Serving

| | | | | | |
|---|---|---|---|---|---|
| Calories: | 231 | Cholesterol: | 43 mg | Vitamin A: | 3,389 IU |
| Fat: | 9.3 gm | Sodium: | 355 mg | Vitamin C: | 95 mg |
| Sat. fat: | 3.1 gm | Fiber: | 3.8 gm | Zinc: | 3.4 mg |
| Iron: | 3.3 mg | Cal. from fat: | 36% | | |

# Shrimp and Rice Salad with Roasted Red Peppers

● This zesty salad will make a beautiful summer luncheon, with herbs from the garden and flavors from France. You may also leave out the shrimp and serve it as a side dish. Either way, the brown rice and red pepper will provide plenty of vitamins E, C, and A.

Preparation time: 20 minutes

Cooking time: 45 minutes

Serves 4

16 ounces medium shrimp, peeled, deveined, and cooked

3 cups cooked brown rice

3 red bell peppers, roasted (see note) and diced

⅓ cup diced red onion

¼ cup (packed) Italian (flat-leaf) parsley, chopped

2 tablespoons chopped fresh thyme leaves

2 tablespoons fresh lemon juice

1 tablespoon extra virgin olive oil

1 tablespoon distilled white vinegar

½ teaspoon Dijon mustard

½ clove garlic, minced

Freshly ground black pepper, to taste

Lettuce leaves, any variety

**1.** In large bowl, combine shrimp, rice, peppers, onion, and parsley. Set aside.

**2.** In small bowl, combine thyme, juice, oil, vinegar, mustard, garlic, and pepper. Whisk vigorously until emulsified. Toss with rice mixture. Serve on lettuce leaves.

## Note:

To roast peppers, heat broiler. Place whole peppers on a foil-lined baking sheet, under broiler, 2 to 3 inches from heat. Turn frequently and roast until skins of peppers are evenly blackened. Close foil around the peppers so the steam cannot escape. Allow the peppers to cool this way for at least 20 minutes. Peel, core, and seed the peppers with a sharp paring knife.

*continued*

## Nutrients Per Serving

| | | | | | |
|---|---|---|---|---|---|
| Calories: | 316 | Cholesterol: | 140 mg | Vitamin A: | 3,386 IU |
| Fat: | 6.6 gm | Sodium: | 168 mg | Vitamin C: | 112 mg |
| Sat. fat: | 1 gm | Fiber: | 3.7 gm | Zinc: | 2 mg |
| Iron: | 4 mg | Cal. from fat: | 19% | | |

# Southwestern Chicken and Rice Salad

• If you prefer a vegetarian dish, try replacing the chicken with black beans. The combination of the beans and rice will make a complete protein and the fiber content will go sky high. If you like spice, add a bit more jalapeño. Hot peppers are some of the best sources of vitamin C.

Preparation time: 25 minutes

Cooking time: 45 minutes

Serves 4

| | |
|---|---|
| 2 cups diced cooked chicken breast | ¼ cup (packed) fresh cilantro leaves, chopped |
| 2 cups cooked brown rice | 1 jalapeño pepper, seeded and minced |
| ½ ripe avocado, peeled, pitted, and diced | 1 teaspoon ground cumin |
| 2 cups diced tomato | 2 tablespoons fresh lime juice |
| ½ red bell pepper, seeded and diced | 4 teaspoons safflower oil |
| ½ cup diced onion | Tabasco or other hot sauce, to taste |

1. In large bowl, combine chicken, rice, avocado, tomato, red pepper, onion, cilantro, and jalapeño.

2. In small saucepan, heat cumin over low heat just until fragrant, about 1 minute. Transfer to small bowl along with juice, oil, and hot sauce. Pour over chicken mixture and toss.

*continued*

## Nutrients Per Serving

| | | | | | |
|---|---|---|---|---|---|
| Calories: | 334 | Cholesterol: | 62 mg | Vitamin A: | 1,497 IU |
| Fat: | 11.9 gm | Sodium: | 83 mg | Vitamin C: | 50 mg |
| Sat. fat: | 2.3 gm | Fiber: | 4.3 gm | Zinc: | 2.4 mg |
| Iron: | 2.7 mg | Cal. from fat: | 32% | | |

# Mango and Fennel Salad with Shrimp and Peanuts

• This delightful combination of crisp, smooth, sweet, sour, and spicy makes a refreshing and exotic-tasting meal. Enjoy the taste . . . don't even think about how good it is for you.

Preparation time: 15 minutes

Cooking time: 3 to 4 minutes

Serves 4

| | |
|---|---|
| 24 large shrimp (about 1 pound), peeled and deveined | ¼ cup fresh lime juice |
| 2 mangos, peeled and cut into ⅛-inch slices | 2 tablespoons seasoned rice wine vinegar |
| 2 small fennel bulbs thinly sliced (2 cups) | ½ teaspoon cayenne pepper |
| ¼ cup (packed) fresh cilantro leaves, chopped | Salt, to taste (optional) |
| | ⅓ cup chopped unsalted roasted peanuts (2 ounces) |

**1.** Bring small (1-quart) saucepan of water to a boil over medium heat. Add shrimp and simmer until just cooked through, 3 to 4 minutes. Drain and refresh under cold water. Dry well.

**2.** In medium bowl, combine mangos, fennel, cilantro, juice, vinegar, cayenne, and salt (if used). Mix gently but thoroughly.

**3.** Divide salad among four plates. Arrange shrimp on top. Sprinkle with peanuts and serve immediately.

*continued*

## Nutrients Per Serving

| | | | | | |
|---|---|---|---|---|---|
| Calories: | 266 | Cholesterol: | 140 mg | Vitamin A: | 4,212 IU |
| Fat: | 9 gm | Sodium: | 344 mg | Vitamin C: | 35 mg |
| Sat. fat: | 1.3 gm | Fiber: | 2.9 gm | Zinc: | 2 mg |
| Iron: | 3 mg | Cal. from fat: | 30% | | |

# Tuna Salad Composé

• Here is an antioxidant-rich version of *salade niçoise*, a colorfully composed salad of tuna and vegetables.

Preparation time: 35 minutes

Cooking time: None

Serves 4

2 cups broccoli florets

4 medium carrots, peeled and sliced diagonally (2 cups)

2 cans (6½ ounces each), water-packed tuna

4 anchovy fillets, chopped

½ cup diced tomato

¼ cup (packed) Italian (flat-leaf) parsley leaves, chopped

2 tablespoons fresh lemon juice

1 tablespoon chopped fresh thyme leaves

1 teaspoon red wine vinegar

½ teaspoon grated lemon zest

¼ teaspoon freshly ground black pepper

4 small new potatoes, cooked and sliced

¼ cup thinly sliced red onion

**1.** In a steamer basket, over 1 inch gently boiling water, steam broccoli 2 minutes. Add carrots and steam another 2 minutes until both are crisp-tender. Refresh under cold water and blot dry.

**2.** In small bowl, combine tuna, anchovies, tomato, parsley, juice, thyme, vinegar, zest, and pepper. Toss gently until well combined.

**3.** Place one quarter of tuna mixture in center of each of four plates. Arrange broccoli, carrots, and potatoes around tuna. Sprinkle with onion.

*continued*

## Nutrients Per Serving

| Calories: | 258 | Cholesterol: | 35 mg | Vitamin A: | 16,848 IU |
|---|---|---|---|---|---|
| Fat: | 1.4 gm | Sodium: | 472 mg | Vitamin C: | 80 mg |
| Sat. fat: | .2 gm | Fiber: | 6.5 gm | Zinc: | 1 mg |
| Iron: | 4.9 mg | Cal. from fat: | 5% | | |

# Italian Seafood Salad

- This classic Italian dish is traditionally served as a first course, but it makes a great low-calorie lunch served on a bed of mixed greens.

Preparation time: 35 minutes

Cooking time: 8 minutes

Serves 4

8 ounces medium shrimp, cooked, peeled, deveined, and cut into 1-inch pieces

8 ounces bay scallops, steamed until barely cooked through

4 roasted red bell peppers (see note page 145)

¼ cup sliced pitted green olives

3 tablespoons fresh lemon juice

4 teaspoons extra virgin olive oil

½ cup (packed) Italian (flat-leaf) parsley, chopped

1 tablespoon dried marjoram

2 garlic cloves, bruised with side of knife

18 mussels, well cleaned

1. In large bowl, combine the shrimp, scallops, red peppers, olives, juice, oil, parsley, marjoram, and garlic. Set aside.

2. In large skillet, heat the mussels, covered, until they open. Remove from shells (discarding any that did not open) and toss with seafood mixture. Refrigerate 2 hours or more, and allow salad to come to room temperature before serving.

### Nutrients Per Serving

| | | | | | |
|---|---|---|---|---|---|
| Calories: | 197 | Cholesterol: | 102 mg | Vitamin A: | 3,234 IU |
| Fat: | 7.6 gm | Sodium: | 489 mg | Vitamin C: | 137 mg |
| Sat. fat: | 1 gm | Fiber: | 1.9 gm | Zinc: | 1.8 mg |
| Iron: | 4 mg | Cal. from fat: 35% | | | |

# Chicken–Wild Rice Salad with Mango and Ginger

• This may sound like an unusual combination, but it is sheer heaven. The mango gives the perfect touch of sweetness and the ginger a special zip. The tomato, bell pepper, and orange juice not only add flavor and brilliant color, but also vitamins A and C.

Preparation time: 30 minutes

Cooking time: 45 to 50 minutes

Serves 4

| | |
|---|---|
| 5 cups low-sodium chicken broth, homemade or canned, or water | ¼ cup thinly sliced scallions |
| 1 cup wild rice, rinsed and drained | 2 tablespoons chopped walnuts |
| 2 cups shredded, cooked chicken breast | ⅓ cup orange juice, fresh or from concentrate |
| 2 large ripe mangoes, peeled and diced (2 cups) | 2 tablespoons extra virgin olive oil |
| | 1 teaspoon distilled white vinegar |
| 1 medium tomato, diced | 1½ teaspoons grated fresh ginger |
| 1 red bell pepper, seeded and diced | ½ teaspoon freshly ground black pepper |
| 1 cup diced cucumber | Salt, to taste (optional) |

**1.** In medium (2-quart saucepan), bring broth or water to boil. Stir in the wild rice, reduce heat to low, and simmer, uncovered, until tender, about 45 minutes. Drain well and cool to room temperature.

**2.** In large bowl, combine rice, chicken, mango, tomato, red pepper, cucumber, scallions, and walnuts.

**3.** In separate bowl, combine juice, oil, vinegar, ginger, pepper, and salt (if used). Toss with the mango mixture.

## Nutrients Per Serving

| | | | | | |
|---|---|---|---|---|---|
| Calories: | 447 | Cholesterol: | 62 mg | Vitamin A: | 4,561 IU |
| Fat: | 14 gm | Sodium: | 252 mg | Vitamin C: | 74 mg |
| Sat. fat: | 2.6 gm | Fiber: | 2.8 gm | Zinc: | 4 mg |
| Iron: | 1.4 mg | Cal. from fat: | 28% | | |

# Pasta, Broccoli, and Basil Salad

• Flavors of the Mediterranean come through in this simple yet delicious pasta salad. It is beautiful as well, accented with the bright red of the pepper and green of the broccoli. Perfect for the buffet table—and loaded with vitamins, fiber, and iron.

Preparation time: 20 minutes

Cooking time: Pasta cooking time

Serves 4

| | |
|---|---|
| 12 ounces spiral pasta | ½ cup crumbled feta cheese |
| 4 cups broccoli florets | 1 tablespoon extra virgin olive oil |
| 2 red bell peppers, seeded and thinly slivered | ¼ teaspoon freshly ground black pepper |
| ¼ cup slivered red onion | 1 cup (packed) fresh basil leaves, chopped |
| ¼ cup red wine vinegar | |

1. Cook pasta according to package directions. Add broccoli for last 3 minutes of cooking. Drain pasta and broccoli, reserving ¼ cup cooking liquid.

2. In large bowl, combine red peppers, onion, vinegar, feta, oil, and black pepper.

3. Toss warm pasta, broccoli, and reserved cooking liquid with red pepper mixture. Toss with basil and let stand 30 minutes before serving.

### Nutrients Per Serving

| Calories: | 457 | Cholesterol: | 15 mg | Vitamin A: | 4,588 IU |
|---|---|---|---|---|---|
| Fat: | 9 gm | Sodium: | 229 mg | Vitamin C: | 168 mg |
| Sat. fat: | 3.2 gm | Fiber: | 7.3 gm | Zinc: | 1.8 mg |
| Iron: | 6.5 mg | Cal. from fat: | 18% | | |

Chapter 10

....................

# Side Dishes

Among these recipes are lots of vegetable and grain side dishes that boast generous amounts of antioxidants yet are stylish enough to tempt the finicky palates of the nonvegetable lover in your family. Every single entry contains both vitamin C *and* beta-carotene, but some, like the Baked Sweet Potato Fries and the Roasted Butternut Squash and Garlic Puree, are exceptionally rich in the two nutrients. One of my favorite side dishes, Carrot and Prune Tzimmes, has about six times the Recommended Daily Value for Vitamin A (most of it as beta-carotene). But the reason my family gobbles these up has to do with taste rather than nutrient profile.

You may notice that the percentage of calories from fat seems a bit high on a few of these dishes, but not to worry—that's only because the calorie count of the basic ingredients is so low.

# Simple Vegetable Stir-Fry

• Stir frying is a quick and healthy cooking technique. This stir-fry also makes a great meal with brown rice. The basic recipe is flexible, so try adding or substituting other antioxidant-rich vegetables.

Preparation time: 10 minutes

Cooking time: 5 to 7 minutes

Serves 4

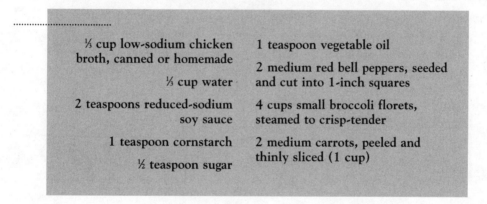

⅓ cup low-sodium chicken broth, canned or homemade

⅓ cup water

2 teaspoons reduced-sodium soy sauce

1 teaspoon cornstarch

½ teaspoon sugar

1 teaspoon vegetable oil

2 medium red bell peppers, seeded and cut into 1-inch squares

4 cups small broccoli florets, steamed to crisp-tender

2 medium carrots, peeled and thinly sliced (1 cup)

**1.** In small bowl, combine broth, soy sauce, cornstarch, and sugar. Mix well.

**2.** In large nonstick skillet, heat oil over high heat. Add red peppers and cook 3 minutes, stirring constantly. Add chicken broth mixture, broccoli, and carrots. Continue cooking, stirring constantly, 1 minute. Cover and continue cooking until vegetables are tender, about 2 minutes.

| Nutrients Per Serving | | | | | |
|---|---|---|---|---|---|
| Calories: | 65 | Cholesterol: | 0 | Vitamin A: | 11,201 IU |
| Fat: | 1.6 gm | Sodium: | 187 mg | Vitamin C: | 155 mg |
| Sat. fat: | .2 gm | Fiber: | 3.9 gm | Zinc: | .5 mg |
| Iron: | 1.2 mg | Cal. from fat: | 23% | | |

# Baked Sweet Potato Fries

• These fries are a low-fat and healthy alternative to french fries. The children will love the sweet taste. Don't mention that they are healthy and everyone will dig in.

Preparation time: 10 minutes

Cooking time: 30 to 35 minutes

Serves 4

| | |
|---|---|
| 4 sweet potatoes (8 ounces each), scrubbed | ⅛ teaspoon cayenne pepper (optional) |
| 1 teaspoon olive oil | Salt, to taste (optional) |

1.   Preheat oven to 450°F.

2.   Cut unpeeled potatoes lengthwise into ⅓-inch slices. Cut into sticks. In large bowl, combine oil and cayenne. Add potatoes and toss until well coated.

3.   Transfer potatoes to baking sheet coated with nonstick cooking spray. Bake 15 minutes; turn and continue cooking until golden, 15 to 20 minutes. Sprinkle with salt (if used).

### Nutrients Per Serving

| Calories: | 250 | Cholesterol: | 0 | Vitamin A: | 45,503 IU |
|---|---|---|---|---|---|
| Fat: | 2 gm | Sodium: | 29 mg | Vitamin C: | 52 mg |
| Sat. fat: | .3 gm | Fiber: | 6.8 gm | Zinc: | .6 mg |
| Iron: | 1.3 mg | Cal. from fat: | 7% | | |

# Roasted Butternut Squash and Garlic Puree

• This puree can also be made in the food processor, but I prefer the chunky-smooth texture that a ricer or food mill creates. Feel free to make it by hand as I do, or with a machine for a smooth puree.

Preparation time: 10 minutes

Cooking time: 50 minutes

Serves 4

1 butternut squash (2 pounds), halved and seeded

2 cloves garlic, unpeeled

2 teaspoons unsalted butter

½ teaspoon chopped fresh sage leaves

¼ teaspoon cayenne pepper

¼ teaspoon grated nutmeg

Salt, to taste (optional)

**1.** Preheat oven to 375°F.

**2.** Place squash, cut side down, in baking pan. Bake until tender, about 50 minutes. After 25 minutes, wrap garlic cloves in foil. Place them alongside squash for last 25 minutes of cooking.

**3.** Remove squash pulp from peel. Squeeze garlic from skins. Run squash pulp and garlic through food mill or ricer into large bowl.

**4.** Add butter, sage, cayenne, nutmeg, and salt (if used). Stir well.

### Nutrients Per Serving

| | | | | | |
|---|---|---|---|---|---|
| Calories: | 106 | Cholesterol: | 5 mg | Vitamin A: | 14,992 IU |
| Fat: | 2 gm | Sodium: | 8 mg | Vitamin C: | 41 mg |
| Sat. fat: | 1.3 gm | Fiber: | 5 gm | Zinc: | .3 mg |
| Iron: | 1.4 mg | Cal. from fat: | 17% | | |

# Carrot and Prune Tzimmes

• *Tzimmes* is a Yiddish word that means "a bit of this and a bit of that." There are hundreds of versions around the world. Here is mine. This sweet treat, full of beta-carotene and fiber, is sure to be a favorite with kids and grownups alike.

Preparation time: 12 minutes

Cooking time: 32 minutes

Serves 4

| | |
|---|---|
| 2 teaspoons safflower oil | ⅓ cup (packed) light brown sugar |
| 1 cup chopped onion | ½ teaspoon grated orange zest |
| 1 pound carrots, peeled and sliced diagonally ¼ inch thick (4 cups) | ½ teaspoon freshly ground black pepper |
| 8 prunes, chopped | 1 tablespoon fresh lemon juice |
| ⅔ cup water | ½ teaspoon chopped fresh rosemary leaves |
| ½ cup orange juice, fresh or from concentrate | Salt, to taste |

1. In medium (2-quart) saucepan, heat oil over medium heat. Add onion and cook, stirring occasionally, until tender, 4 to 5 minutes. Add carrots and cook, stirring, 3 minutes.

2. Stir in prunes, water, orange juice, brown sugar, zest, and pepper. Simmer, covered, until mixture is thick and carrots are tender, 20 to 25 minutes.

3. Remove from heat and stir in lemon juice, rosemary, and salt.

### Nutrients Per Serving

| | | | | | |
|---|---|---|---|---|---|
| Calories: | 207 | Cholesterol: | 0 | Vitamin A: | 31,303 |
| Fat: | 2.6 gm | Sodium: | 49 mg | Vitamin C: | 27 mg |
| Sat. fat: | .5 gm | Fiber: | 5.5 gm | Zinc: | .4 mg |
| Iron: | 1.5 mg | Cal. from fat: | 11% | | |

# Ginger-braised Cabbage

•   The pure flavors of ginger and cabbage blend beautifully in this lovely braised dish. Try to keep the cabbage wedges from falling apart. Whole pieces make the best presentation.

Preparation time: 5 minutes

Cooking time: 25 minutes

Serves 6

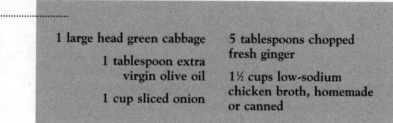

1 large head green cabbage

1 tablespoon extra virgin olive oil

1 cup sliced onion

5 tablespoons chopped fresh ginger

1½ cups low-sodium chicken broth, homemade or canned

**1.**   Cut cabbage through core into 12 wedges. The pieces should remain intact. Set aside.

**2.**   Heat oil in large (6-quart) saucepan over medium heat. Add onion and ginger and cook, stirring, 1 minute. Stir broth into mixture.

**3.**   Carefully stand cabbage wedges in saucepan, cover, and cook until cabbage is tender, about 20 minutes. Arrange wedges on platter or plates. Spoon onion and ginger on top.

| Nutrients Per Serving | | | | | |
|---|---|---|---|---|---|
| Calories: | 94 | Cholesterol: | 0 | Vitamin A: | 286 IU |
| Fat: | 3 gm | Sodium: | 202 mg | Vitamin C: | 109 mg |
| Sat. fat: | .4 gm | Fiber: | 5.9 gm | Zinc: | .5 mg |
| Iron: | 1.3 mg | Cal. from fat: | 29% | | |

# Garlic-sautéed Sweet and Hot Peppers

• All peppers are high in vitamin C, so use any combination that you like. I love the Hungarian hot peppers because they are spicy, but not burning. Try serving these peppers over a grilled piece of meat or chicken.

Preparation time: 15 minutes

Cooking time: 22 minutes

Serves 4

| | |
|---|---|
| 2 teaspoons olive oil | 3 cloves garlic, slivered |
| 1 cup sliced onion | ¼ cup (packed) fresh basil leaves, slivered |
| 2 red bell peppers, seeded and sliced | 1 tablespoon balsamic vinegar |
| 2 Italian frying peppers, seeded and sliced | ¼ teaspoon freshly ground black pepper, or more to taste |
| 1 Hungarian hot pepper, seeded and slivered, or 1 jalapeño pepper, seeded and minced | Salt, to taste (optional) |

1. In large nonstick skillet, heat oil over medium-high heat. Add onion and cook, stirring, until wilted, about 4 minutes.

2. Add the peppers and garlic and continue cooking, stirring occasionally, for 3 minutes. Add water, reduce heat to medium-low, cover, and cook until peppers are tender, about 15 minutes.

3. Toss in basil, vinegar, pepper, and salt (if used). Serve hot.

| Nutrients Per Serving | | | | | |
| --- | --- | --- | --- | --- | --- |
| Calories: | 65 | Cholesterol: | 0 | Vitamin A: | 2,460 IU |
| Fat: | 2.5 gm | Sodium: | 5 mg | Vitamin C: | 151 mg |
| Sat. fat: | .3 gm | Fiber: | 1.6 gm | Zinc: | .7 mg |
| Iron: | 1.2 mg | Cal. from fat: | 35% | | |

# Molasses-braised Collard Greens

• A touch of molasses gives a sweet bite to this healthful version of a classic Southern dish.

Preparation time: 15 minutes

Cooking time: 52 minutes

Serves 4

| | |
|---|---|
| 1 bunch collard greens (1¼ pounds), thick stems removed | 2 tablespoons light molasses |
| 1 tablespoon canola oil | 1½ teaspoons Tabasco or other hot sauce |
| 1½ cups sliced onion | ¼ teaspoon freshly ground black pepper |
| 2 cloves garlic, minced | Salt, to taste |
| ¼ cup water | |

**1.** Rinse, but do not dry collards. Cut into 1-inch strips.

**2.** In large nonstick skillet, heat oil over medium heat. Add onion and garlic; cook, stirring, until golden, about 8 to 10 minutes.

**3.** Meanwhile, in small bowl, stir together the water, molasses, and hot sauce.

**4.** Stir collards into skillet. Add molasses mixture and stir gently. Reduce heat to low and cook, covered, 40 minutes, stirring occasionally. Add salt and pepper.

### Nutrients Per Serving

| Calories: | 152 | Cholesterol: | 0 | Vitamin A: | 2,964 IU |
|---|---|---|---|---|---|
| Fat: | 4 gm | Sodium: | 48 mg | Vitamin C: | 35 mg |
| Sat. fat: | .8 gm | Fiber: | 4 gm | Zinc: | .4 mg |
| Iron: | .6 mg | Cal. from fat: | 24% | | |

# Sautéed Broccoli with Garlic

• Sometimes the simplest things are the best. In this recipe, the broccoli is almost dry sautéed, keeping the broccoli fresh and crisp and low in calories. The bright green vegetable, scattered with golden slivers of crisp garlic, will be an elegant accompaniment to any meal.

Preparation time: 5 minutes

Cooking time: 5 minutes

Serves 4

2 teaspoons olive oil

4 cloves garlic, finely slivered

4 cups broccoli florets and peeled stems, steamed to crisp-tender

Salt, to taste (optional)

Freshly ground black pepper, to taste

1. In large nonstick skillet, heat oil over medium heat. Add garlic and cook, stirring constantly, for 30 seconds.

2. Add broccoli and continue cooking until garlic is golden.

3. Toss with salt (if used) and pepper. Remove from heat.

| Nutrients Per Serving | | | | | |
|---|---|---|---|---|---|
| Calories: | 49 | Cholesterol: | 0 | Vitamin A: | 1,357 IU |
| Fat: | 2.6 gm | Sodium: | 24 mg | Vitamin C: | 83 mg |
| Sat. fat: | .3 gm | Fiber: | 2.5 gm | Zinc: | .4 mg |
| Iron: | .8 mg | Cal. from fat: | 47% | | |

# Spinach Cheese Gratin

- This classic dish is a sure way to get the children to eat their spinach. Try it with Swiss chard as well. Either version is a great source of vitamin A.

Preparation time: 8 minutes

Cooking time: 25 minutes

Serves 4

1 pound cleaned, destemmed spinach leaves, rinsed but not dried

1½ ounces Jarlsberg cheese, coarsely grated

1 tablespoon grated parmesan cheese

1 clove garlic, minced

⅛ teaspoon freshly ground black pepper

**1.** Preheat oven to 400°F. Spray 1-quart casserole with nonstick cooking spray.

**2.** Heat large nonstick skillet over high heat. Add damp spinach and cook, tossing gently, until wilted, 2 to 3 minutes.

**3.** Place half of spinach in prepared casserole. Sprinkle with half Jarlsberg, half parmesan, half garlic, and half pepper. Top with remaining spinach, sprinkle with remaining cheeses, garlic, and pepper.

**4.** Bake on top shelf of oven until cheeses are melted and bubbly, 20 minutes.

### Nutrients Per Serving

| | | | | | |
|---|---|---|---|---|---|
| Calories: | 70 | Cholesterol: | 8 mg | Vitamin A: | 7,668 IU |
| Fat: | 3.6 gm | Sodium: | 164 mg | Vitamin C: | 32 mg |
| Sat. fat: | .3 gm | Fiber: | 3 gm | Zinc: | .6 mg |
| Iron: | 3 mg | Cal. from fat: | 46% | | |

# Turnip-Potato Puree

• There are few things more comforting than a nice puree. Try this dish in the winter when we all need some comfort and a lot of vitamin C.

Preparation time: 5 minutes

Cooking time: 15 minutes

Serves 4

3 purple-top turnips (1½ pounds), peeled and cut into 1-inch pieces

2 large all-purpose potatoes (1¼ pounds) peeled and cut into 1-inch pieces

¾ cup (packed) fresh Italian (flat-leaf) parsley, chopped

2 tablespoons sour cream

½ teaspoon freshly ground black pepper

⅛ teaspoon grated nutmeg

Salt, to taste (optional)

**1.** In steamer basket, steam turnips over 1 inch gently boiling water until tender, 10 to 15 minutes. Meanwhile, in separate saucepan of boiling water, boil potatoes until tender, 10 to 15 minutes. Drain both well.

**2.** Transfer the turnips and potatoes to food processor. Add parsley, sour cream, pepper, nutmeg, and salt (if used). Puree until smooth.

| *Nutrients Per Serving* | | | | | |
|---|---|---|---|---|---|
| Calories: | 139 | Cholesterol: | 2 mg | Vitamin A: | 636 IU |
| Fat: | 1.3 gm | Sodium: | 110 mg | Vitamin C: | 60 mg |
| Sat. fat: | .8 gm | Fiber: | 4.7 gm | Zinc: | .5 mg |
| Iron: | 2 mg | Cal. from fat: | 8% | | |

# Wild Rice with Oranges and Scallions

• This wild rice dish is a long time favorite with my family. The sweet tartness of the oranges balances the nutty flavor of the rice. It also provides a complement of vitamin C to the rice's selenium.

Preparation time: 10 minutes

Cooking time: 55 to 60 minutes

Serves 4

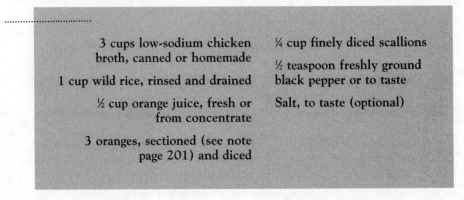

3 cups low-sodium chicken broth, canned or homemade

1 cup wild rice, rinsed and drained

½ cup orange juice, fresh or from concentrate

3 oranges, sectioned (see note page 201) and diced

¼ cup finely diced scallions

½ teaspoon freshly ground black pepper or to taste

Salt, to taste (optional)

**1.**   In medium (2-quart) saucepan, combine broth and rice. Bring to boil over medium-high heat. Reduce heat to low and simmer, uncovered, until tender, about 45 minutes. Drain well.

**2.**   Add juice to rice. Heat over medium heat, stirring gently until liquid is absorbed, 5 to 7 minutes. Remove from heat. Toss in oranges, scallions, and pepper. If desired, add salt to taste.

### Nutrients Per Serving

| Calories: | 226 | Cholesterol: | 0 | Vitamin A: | 283 IU |
|---|---|---|---|---|---|
| Fat: | 1.2 gm | Sodium: | 324 mg | Vitamin C: | 64 mg |
| Sat. fat: | tr | Fiber: | 5 gm | Zinc: | 2.5 mg |
| Iron: | 1 mg | Cal. from fat: | 5% | | |

# Brown Rice with Vegetables and Almonds

• This rice pilaf, with its hints of the Middle East, features the warm flavors of cumin and cinnamon, brightened with the finishing burst of lemon juice and a sprinkle of parsley.

Preparation time: 10 minutes

Cooking time: 50 minutes

Serves 4

2 teaspoons safflower oil

1 cup chopped onion

1 cup diced carrots

½ cup diced green or red bell pepper

1 clove garlic, minced

1 tablespoon ground cumin

1 cup brown rice

1½ cups reduced-sodium chicken broth, canned or homemade, or water

½ cup orange juice, fresh or from concentrate

½ teaspoon ground cinnamon

¼ teaspoon salt

½ cup (packed) Italian (flat-leaf) parsley leaves, chopped

4 teaspoons fresh lemon juice

¼ cup slivered almonds (optional), toasted

**1.** Heat oil in large (3-quart) wide saucepan over medium heat. Add onion, carrots, bell peppers, garlic, and cumin and cook, stirring frequently, for 3 minutes. Add rice; stir until coated with oil.

**2.** Stir in broth or water, orange juice, cinnamon, and salt; bring to a boil, then cover, reduce heat to low and simmer until tender, about 45 minutes.

**3.** Remove rice from heat. Add parsley, lemon juice, and almonds (if used). Mix well.

*continued*

## Note:

To toast almonds, spread slivered almonds in a jelly roll pan and toast until fragrant and lightly golden, about 10 minutes.

### Nutrients Per Serving

| Calories: | 284 | Cholesterol: | 0 | Vitamin A: | 8,249 IU |
|-----------|-----|--------------|---|------------|----------|
| Fat: | 7 gm | Sodium: | 398 mg | Vitamin C: | 37 mg |
| Sat. fat: | .8 gm | Fiber: | 3.9 gm | Zinc: | 1.7 mg |
| Iron: | 2.6 mg | Cal. from fat: | 22% | | |

# Wheatberry Sauté

• This beautiful side dish will be a welcome addition to any plate, with its muted colors, subtle flavors, and satisfying crunch. Grain lovers take note: Wheatberries are higher in protein and less caloric than rice or couscous.

Preparation time: 10 minutes

Cooking time: 50 minutes

Serves 4

| | |
|---|---|
| 4 cups water | ½ cup chopped dried apricots (3 ounces) |
| ¾ cup wheatberries | ½ cup water |
| 2 teaspoons safflower oil | ⅓ cup (packed) fresh basil leaves, chopped |
| 1 cup chopped onion | |
| ⅓ cup slivered almonds (optional) | ½ teaspoon freshly ground black pepper |
| 2 cloves garlic, minced | Salt, to taste (optional) |
| 1 cup diced tomato | |

1.   In a medium (2-quart) saucepan, bring water to boil. Add wheatberries and return to boil, then reduce heat to low, cover, and simmer 45 minutes, or to desired tenderness. Drain well.

2.   In large nonstick skillet, heat oil over medium-high heat. Add onion and cook, stirring frequently, until wilted, 4 to 5 minutes. Add almonds (if used) and garlic and cook until almonds are toasted, 2 to 3 minutes.

3.   Add tomato and apricots. Stir gently. Add water and cook until absorbed, 3 to 4 minutes. Remove from heat. Toss with basil, pepper, and salt (if used).

*continued*

### Nutrients Per Serving

| Calories: | 217 | Cholesterol: | 0 | Vitamin A: | 1592 IU |
|---|---|---|---|---|---|
| Fat: | 5.4 gm | Sodium: | 12 mg | Vitamin C: | 13 mg |
| Sat. fat: | .6 gm | Fiber: | 2.7 gm | Zinc: | .6 mg |
| Iron: | 3.3 mg | Cal. from fat: 22% | | | |

Chapter 11

# Side Salads

Cool and refreshing, colorful salads are perfect first courses for a company dinner. Better yet, what's left over can easily fit into your lunchbox for the next day, keeping your at-work diet rich in antioxidants. I'm partial to the Carrot-Papaya Coleslaw for family picnics and as a side dish for any kind of sandwich. It's lower in fat than traditional coleslaw but you'll be so bowled over by the lush tropical papaya flavor that you won't even notice. And when you need a potato salad that will wow the tastebuds, try either the Potato and Roasted Red Pepper Salad or the Rosemary–Sweet Potato Salad. Traditional potato salads yield little in the way of antioxidant nutrients, but these two selections, due to the inclusion of red peppers and sweet potatoes, are rich in both beta-carotene and vitamin C.

You may notice that the percentage of calories from fat seems a bit high on some of these salads, but the actual amount of fat, in grams, is quite moderate. This peculiarity arises from the fact that most salad ingredients are so low in calories.

# Spinach Salad with Fresh Raspberry Vinaigrette

• Now here's an intriguing combination—fresh, crisp spinach leaves bathed in raspberries and balsamic vinegar, sprinkled with crisp slivers of smoky bacon.

Preparation time: 10 minutes

Cooking time: 8 to 10 minutes

Serves 4

| | |
|---|---|
| 2 strips bacon, chopped | Salt, to taste (optional) |
| 1 cup fresh raspberries | 4 cups (packed) spinach leaves (2 pounds before stems removed), well rinsed and dried |
| ¼ cup balsamic vinegar | |
| 4 teaspoons extra virgin olive oil | |
| ¼ teaspoon freshly ground black pepper | ½ cup thinly sliced red onion |

1. In medium nonstick skillet, cook bacon until crisp, 8 to 10 minutes. Drain on paper towels.

2. In small bowl, combine raspberries, vinegar, oil, pepper, and salt (if used). With back of fork, gently crush raspberries until they are just broken up.

3. Divide the spinach among four plates, drizzle with raspberry dressing, and sprinkle with onion and bacon bits.

| Nutrients Per Serving | | | | | |
|---|---|---|---|---|---|
| Calories: | 99 | Cholesterol: | 3 mg | Vitamin A: | 4,749 IU |
| Fat: | 6.6 gm | Sodium: | 109 mg | Vitamin C: | 31 mg |
| Sat. fat: | 1.3 gm | Fiber: | 3.6 gm | Zinc: | .6 mg |
| Iron: | 2.3 mg | Cal. from fat: | 60% | | |

# Broccoli-Ginger Salad with Soy Almonds

• Asian flavors always work beautifully with broccoli. This salad is bright tasting, refreshing, and bursting with vitamin C. The soy-flavored almonds not only provide a great flavor contrast, but also a sprinkling of vitamin E.

Preparation time: 20 minutes

Cooking time: 3 to 4 minutes

Serves 4

| | |
|---|---|
| 12 almonds (1 ounce), cut into 4 pieces each | 1 teaspoon grated lemon zest |
| 2½ teaspoons safflower oil | 1 teaspoon freshly ground black pepper |
| 2½ teaspoons reduced-sodium soy sauce | ½ clove garlic, minced |
| 2 tablespoons fresh lemon juice | 4 cups small broccoli florets, steamed to crisp-tender |
| 2 tablespoons seasoned rice wine vinegar | 3 scallions, cut in thin diagonal slivers (⅓ cup) |
| 2 teaspoons grated fresh ginger | |

**1.** Heat medium nonstick skillet over medium heat. Add almonds and ½ teaspoon of the oil. Cook, stirring frequently, until just toasted, 3 to 4 minutes. Add 2 teaspoons of the soy sauce and stir until coated, about 1 minute. Remove nuts from pan; set aside to cool.

**2.** In medium bowl, whisk together juice, vinegar, remaining 2 teaspoons oil, ginger, zest, pepper, remaining ½ teaspoon soy sauce, and garlic.

**3.** Toss broccoli and scallions with dressing. Sprinkle with nuts.

## Nutrients Per Serving

| Calories: | 125 | Cholesterol: | 0 | Vitamin A: | 2,086 IU |
|-----------|-----|--------------|---|------------|----------|
| Fat: | 6.7 gm | Sodium: | 309 mg | Vitamin C: | 98 mg |
| Sat. fat: | .5 gm | Fiber: | 5.6 gm | Zinc: | .3 mg |
| Iron: | 1.6 mg | Cal. from fat: | 48% | | |

# Southwestern Carrot and Apple Salad

- The sweet, sour, and spicy dressing here is a welcome change from the traditional mayonnaise-based topping that is usually served with carrot and apples.

Preparation time: 10 minutes

Cooking time: 1 minute

Serves 4

1 teaspoon ground cumin

1 tablespoon fresh lime juice

1 tablespoon safflower oil

¼ teaspoon salt (optional)

3 dashes Tabasco or other hot sauce

2 cups grated carrots (4 to 5 carrots)

1 green apple, cored and grated (1 cup)

3 tablespoons chopped fresh cilantro leaves

¼ cup raisins

**1.** In small skillet, heat cumin over low heat just until fragrant, about 1 minute. Remove from heat.

**2.** In small bowl, whisk together cumin, juice, oil, salt (if used), and hot sauce.

**3.** In large bowl, combine carrots, apple, cilantro, and raisins. Toss with dressing.

### Nutrients Per Serving

| Calories: | 100 | Cholesterol: | 0 | Vitamin A: | 15,514 IU |
|---|---|---|---|---|---|
| Fat: | 3.7 gm | Sodium: | 26 mg | Vitamin C: | 7 mg |
| Sat. fat: | .3 gm | Fiber: | 2.8 gm | Zinc: | .2 mg |
| Iron: | .8 mg | Cal. from fat: | 33% | | |

# Carrot-Papaya Coleslaw

• This sweet and spicy salad is nothing like the old standby. Regular coleslaw is transformed into a tropical treat with a tantalizing mix of flavors and textures.

Preparation time: 12 minutes

Cooking time: None

Serves 4

2 cups shredded green cabbage

2 medium carrots, grated (1 cup)

1 red bell pepper, seeded and thinly slivered

1 papaya, peeled, seeded, and slivered

¼ cup reduced-fat mayonnaise

⅓ cup (packed) fresh cilantro leaves, chopped

2 tablespoons fresh lemon juice

½ to 1 roasted jalapeño pepper (see note, page 145), finely minced

1 clove garlic, minced

¼ teaspoon freshly ground black pepper

1. In large bowl, combine cabbage, carrots, red pepper, and papaya. Set aside.

2. In small bowl, combine mayonnaise, cilantro, lemon juice, jalapeño, garlic, and black pepper. Add to cabbage mixture. Toss well.

### Nutrients Per Serving

| | | | | | |
|---|---|---|---|---|---|
| Calories: | 100 | Cholesterol: | 5 mg | Vitamin A: | 10,426 IU |
| Fat: | 4.3 gm | Sodium: | 102 mg | Vitamin C: | 111 mg |
| Sat. fat: | 1 gm | Fiber: | 2.7 gm | Zinc: | <1 mg |
| Iron: | <1 mg | Cal. from fat: | 39% | | |

# Asparagus Salad Vinaigrette

• This recipe is so simple, yet so delicious. Crisp peppers and delicate asparagus are elegantly dressed with a gentle vinaigrette. Buy a high-quality balsamic vinegar—it will make all the difference in your salads.

Preparation time: 10 minutes, plus 30 minutes marination

Cooking time: 5 to 7 minutes

Serves 4

24 asparagus spears, trimmed

1 red bell pepper, seeded and thinly slivered

¼ cup thinly sliced red onion

3 tablespoons balsamic vinegar

1 teaspoon extra virgin olive oil

1 clove garlic, crushed through a press

¼ teaspoon freshly ground black pepper

1. In steamer basket, steam asparagus over 1 inch gently boiling water until tender, 5 to 7 minutes. Transfer to serving platter.

2. Meanwhile, in small bowl, combine red pepper, onion, vinegar, oil, garlic, and black pepper.

3. Pour dressing over asparagus. Let marinate 30 minutes before serving.

### Nutrients Per Serving

| Calories: | 41 | Cholesterol: | 0 | Vitamin A: | 1,840 IU |
|---|---|---|---|---|---|
| Fat: | 1.4 gm | Sodium: | 4 mg | Vitamin C: | 65 mg |
| Sat. fat: | .2 gm | Fiber: | 1.4 gm | Zinc: | .6 mg |
| Iron: | .8 mg | Cal. from fat: | 31% | | |

# Potato and Roasted Red Pepper Salad

• This is a hearty salad that goes well with grilled beef or chicken. Bring it to a picnic for a mayonnaise-free and antioxidant-rich alternative to the high-fat classic.

Preparation time: 15 minutes, plus 30 minutes marination

Cooking time: 20 to 25 minutes

Serves 4

| | |
|---|---|
| 1 pound all-purpose potatoes, scrubbed | 1 tablespoon chopped fresh rosemary or thyme leaves |
| 4 red bell peppers, roasted (see note, page 145) | 2 teaspoons Dijon mustard |
| ½ cup sliced sweet white onion | 1 clove garlic, crushed through a press |
| ½ cup (packed) Italian (flat-leaf) parsley leaves, chopped | ½ teaspoon freshly ground black pepper |
| 2 tablespoons white wine vinegar | Salt, to taste (optional) |
| 1 tablespoon extra virgin olive oil | |

1. In large (3-quart) saucepan of cold water, bring potatoes to a boil and boil until tender, 20–25 minutes. When cool enough to handle, slice potatoes ⅛ inch thick.

2. In large bowl, combine potatoes, peppers, and onion. Set aside.

3. In a separate bowl or mini-processor, combine parsley, vinegar, oil, rosemary, mustard, garlic, pepper, and salt (if used). Mix well, either by whisking or pureeing.

4. Add dressing to potato mixture and toss gently, until well coated. Set aside until completely cooled, about 30 minutes.

*continued*

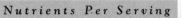

**Nutrients Per Serving**

| Calories: | 151 | Cholesterol: | 0 | Vitamin A: | 3,179 IU |
|-----------|-----|--------------|------|------------|----------|
| Fat: | 4 gm | Sodium: | 90 mg | Vitamin C: | 156 mg |
| Sat. fat: | .6 gm | Fiber: | 4.1 gm | Zinc: | .1 mg |
| Iron: | 2.6 mg | Cal. from fat: | 24% | | |

# Fennel and Orange Salad with Parsley and Olives

• This salad is a Mediterranean classic. Crisp fennel is beautifully contrasted with succulent orange and sultry olives. The oranges and parsley provide tremendous vitamin C.

Preparation time: 12 minutes

Cooking time: None

Serves 4

1 fennel bulb, halved and thinly sliced

4 navel oranges, sectioned (see note page 201)

½ cup (packed) Italian (flat-leaf) parsley leaves, chopped

2 tablespoons orange juice, fresh or from concentrate

4 teaspoons extra virgin olive oil

8 cured green olives, pitted and slivered

1 teaspoon grated orange zest

¼ teaspoon freshly ground black pepper

Salt, to taste (optional)

In medium bowl, combine fennel, oranges, parsley, juice, oil, olives, zest, pepper, and salt (if used). Toss well.

**Nutrients Per Serving**

| Calories: | 129 | Cholesterol: | 0 | Vitamin A: | 735 IU |
|-----------|-----|--------------|-----|------------|--------|
| Fat: | 5.9 gm | Sodium: | 243 mg | Vitamin C: | 96 mg |
| Sat. fat: | .8 gm | Fiber: | 4.5 gm | Zinc: | .2 mg |
| Iron: | 1.3 mg | Cal. from fat: | 41% | | |

# Rosemary–Sweet Potato Salad

• The combination of sweet potatoes and rosemary is exquisite. But this salad does not just taste delicious, it is rich in antioxidants, too. Beta-carotene from the sweet potatoes, vitamin C from the peppers, and E from the nuts.

Preparation time: 15 minutes

Cooking time: 45 minutes, for potatoes

Serves 4

| | |
|---|---|
| 2 tablespoons currants | 1 teaspoon lemon zest |
| ½ cup hot water | 2 tablespoons fresh lemon juice |
| 1½ pounds sweet potatoes, baked, peeled, and diced | 4 teaspoons safflower oil |
| 1 red bell pepper, seeded and thinly slivered | 2 teaspoons chopped fresh rosemary leaves |
| ½ cup thinly sliced red onion | ¼ cup sliced almonds, toasted (see note page 172) |
| ¼ cup (packed) Italian (flat-leaf) parsley leaves, chopped | |

**1.** In small bowl, combine currants and water. Set aside 10 minutes. Drain well.

**2.** In large bowl, combine sweet potatoes, red pepper, onion, parsley, zest, and currants.

**3.** In small bowl, whisk together juice, oil, and rosemary. Toss gently with potato mixture. Sprinkle with almonds.

### Nutrients Per Serving

| Calories: | 225 | Cholesterol: | 0 | Vitamin A: | 25,852 IU |
|---|---|---|---|---|---|
| Fat: | 8 gm | Sodium: | 20 mg | Vitamin C: | 69 mg |
| Sat. fat: | .8 gm | Fiber: | 4.6 gm | Zinc: | .6 mg |
| Iron: | 1.4 mg | Cal. from fat: | 32% | | |

# Summer Tomato Salad

• Every tomato lover has a memory of a hot summer day and the perfect tomato salad. This is it.

Preparation time: 10 minutes, plus 1 hour marination

Cooking time: None

Serves 4

1½ pounds ripe tomatoes, cut in wedges

¾ cup thinly sliced red onion

⅓ cup (packed) fresh basil leaves, shredded

3 tablespoons red wine vinegar

1 tablespoon extra virgin olive oil

¼ teaspoon freshly ground black pepper

Salt, to taste (optional)

**1.** In large bowl, combine tomatoes, onion, and basil; set aside.

**2.** In small bowl, whisk together vinegar, oil, pepper, and salt (if used). Gently toss with tomato mixture. Cover with plastic wrap and set aside 1 hour, stirring once. Do not refrigerate. Serve at room temperature.

### Nutrients Per Serving

| | | | | | |
|---|---|---|---|---|---|
| Calories: | 85 | Cholesterol: | 0 | Vitamin A: | 1,285 IU |
| Fat: | 4 gm | Sodium: | 19 mg | Vitamin C: | 37 mg |
| Sat. fat: | .6 gm | Fiber: | 2.7 gm | Zinc: | .3 mg |
| Iron: | 1.9 mg | Cal. from fat: | 44% | | |

# Chicory Salad with Tomato Caper Dressing

• Chicory is a bitter green for which you must acquire a taste. I have, and I love it served with this robust tomato dressing. Steaming it until just wilted mellows the flavor considerably.

Preparation time: 12 minutes

Cooking time: 1 to 2 minutes

Serves 4

6 cups (packed) bite-sized pieces chicory

2 medium tomatoes, halved and thinly sliced (2 cups)

2 tablespoons chopped capers

4 teaspoons red wine vinegar

1 tablespoon olive oil

2 cloves garlic, minced

¼ teaspoon freshly ground black pepper

**1.** In steamer basket, steam chicory over 1 inch gently boiling water until just wilted, 1 minute.

**2.** In medium bowl, combine tomatoes, capers, vinegar, oil, garlic, and pepper. Whisk vigorously so tomatoes give up their juice.

**3.** Gently toss chicory with dressing. Serve immediately.

### Nutrients Per Serving

| Calories: | 130 | Cholesterol: | 0 | Vitamin A: | 14,060 |
|-----------|-----|--------------|---|------------|--------|
| Fat: | 4.7 gm | Sodium: | 270 mg | Vitamin C: | 99 mg |
| Sat. fat: | .7 gm | Fiber: | 6.6 gm | Zinc: | tr |
| Iron: | 3.5 mg | Cal. from fat: | 32% | | |

# Watercress Salad with Oranges and Grapefruit

• Peppery watercress is beautifully mellowed with fresh citrus fruits. Serve this elegant salad to impress your guests when you entertain, or at family dinners for your health.

Preparation time: 15 minutes

Cooking time: None

Serves 4

1¼ cups orange sections (2 to 3 oranges; see note page 201)

1¼ cups grapefruit sections (see note page 201)

2 tablespoons lime sections (see note page 201)

1 tablespoon extra virgin olive oil

2 cloves garlic, minced

¼ teaspoon freshly ground black pepper

Salt, to taste (optional)

4 cups (packed) watercress, stems trimmed

1. In large bowl, combine ¼ cup each orange and grapefruit sections, the lime, oil, garlic, pepper, and salt (if used). Mix well, breaking up fruit with back of fork.

2. Add remaining fruit and watercress to bowl. Mix gently. Serve immediately.

### Nutrients Per Serving

| Calories: | 90 | Cholesterol: | 0 | Vitamin A: | 2,203 IU |
|---|---|---|---|---|---|
| Fat: | 3.6 gm | Sodium: | 18 mg | Vitamin C: | 75 mg |
| Sat. fat: | .6 gm | Fiber: | 2.8 gm | Zinc: | tr |
| Iron: | .3 mg | Cal. from fat: | 36% | | |

# Minted Cracked Wheat Salad

• Here is an almost classic tabouli salad. I have added some extra vegetables to lower the calories, increase the "crunch," and add some antioxidants. The end result is a wonderfully refreshing summer salad.

Preparation time: 20 to 25 minutes, plus 2 hours marination

Cooking time: None

Serves 4

⅔ cup bulgur (cracked wheat) (4 ounces)

2 cups hot water

2 medium tomatoes, diced (2 cups)

1 cup (packed) Italian (flat-leaf) parsley, chopped

½ cup finely chopped romaine lettuce

⅓ cup thinly sliced scallions

¼ cup chopped fresh mint

1 clove garlic, minced

¼ cup fresh lemon juice, or more to taste

1 tablespoon olive oil

Salt, to taste

**1.** In small bowl, combine bulgur and water. Set aside until softened, 20 to 25 minutes.

**2.** Drain bulgur well, and fluff with a fork. Transfer to large bowl; toss with tomatoes, parsley, lettuce, scallion, mint, and garlic.

**3.** In small bowl, combine ¼ cup lemon juice, olive oil, and salt. Whisk well. Toss dressing with bulgur mixture. Refrigerate at least 2 hours before serving. If desired, add more lemon juice to taste.

| Calories: | 158 | Cholesterol: | 0 | Vitamin A: | 1,684 IU |
|-----------|-----|--------------|---|------------|----------|
| Fat: | 4.3 gm | Sodium: | 24 mg | Vitamin C: | 39 mg |
| Sat. fat: | .6 gm | Fiber: | 7 gm | Zinc: | .8 mg |
| Iron: | 2.3 mg | Cal. from fat: | 24% | | |

## Chapter 12

# Desserts

Whether you're fond of hot desserts, cool custards, or chilling frozen confections, the following assortment of antioxidant-rich sweets is guaranteed to end any meal in style. Elegant and simple, I favor the Cantaloupe Granita with its hefty dose of both beta-carotene and vitamin C. And the Tropical Fruit Salad, rich in these same two nutrients, is a versatile addition to breakfast, lunch, or dinner. But when we crave something warm and delicious, the Sweet Potato Custard or the Spice-poached Fruit Compote hit the spot. The custard, loaded with beta-carotene, has only 1 gram of fat per serving and a generous dose of calcium. And the poached fruit, which contains both vitamin C and beta-carotene, delivers nearly 7 grams of fiber per serving!

# Spice-poached Fruit Compote

• This fruit compote is perfect for a winter's evening. Try experimenting with other dried fruit as well. Many stores are now stocking dried cherries, nectarines, and even cranberries.

Preparation time: 10 minutes

Cooking time: 30 to 35 minutes

Serves 4

| | |
|---|---|
| 1 cup orange juice, fresh or from concentrate | 1 dried hot red pepper |
| ¼ cup fresh lemon juice | 2 pears, peeled, cored, and cut into 8 sections each |
| ½ cup water | 1 tart apple, peeled, cored, and cut into 8 sections |
| 1 cinnamon stick | |
| 5 cloves | 1 cup chopped dried apricots (6 ounces) |
| 2 ¼-inch slices peeled fresh ginger | ¼ cup raisins |

**1.** In a medium (2-quart) saucepan, combine juices, water, cinnamon stick, cloves, ginger, and pepper. Bring mixture to boil, reduce heat to low, and simmer 10 minutes.

**2.** Add pears, apple, apricots, and raisins to saucepan. Simmer until fruit is tender, about 15 minutes.

**3.** Remove fruit from poaching liquid. Strain liquid and return to cleaned saucepan. Boil liquid until it is reduced and syrupy, 6 to 8 minutes. Pour it over fruit. Serve warm or cool.

*continued*

## Nutrients Per Serving

| | | | | | |
|---|---|---|---|---|---|
| Calories: | 230 | Cholesterol: | 0 | Vitamin A: | 3,346 IU |
| Fat: | .8 gm | Sodium: | 10 mg | Vitamin C: | 34 mg |
| Sat. fat: | tr | Fiber: | 6.7 gm | Zinc: | .5 mg |
| Iron: | 2.6 mg | Cal. from fat: | 3% | | |

# Brown Rice and Apricot Pudding

• Who would believe that this rich, sweet pudding is low in fat and so high in vitamin A and fiber? It's pure decadence and no guilt.

Preparation time: 10 minutes

Cooking time: 25 minutes

Serves 6

| | |
|---|---|
| 1 quart low-fat (1%) milk | ½ cup sherry |
| 2 cups cooked brown rice | 3 tablespoons (packed) light brown sugar |
| ¾ cup chopped dried apricots (4½ ounces) | Pinch salt |

**1.** In medium (2-quart) saucepan, combine milk, rice, and salt. Bring to boil over medium heat. Simmer, stirring constantly, until thick, 25 minutes.

**2.** Meanwhile, in small (1-quart) saucepan, combine apricots, sherry, and sugar. Simmer over low heat until apricots are soft and liquid is syrupy, about 5 minutes. Stir into thickened rice mixture. Serve warm or cool.

## Nutrients Per Serving

| Calories: | 299 | Cholesterol: | 6.6 gm | Vitamin A: | 3,284 IU |
|---|---|---|---|---|---|
| Fat: | 2.2 gm | Sodium: | 114 mg | Vitamin C: | 3 mg |
| Sat. fat: | 1.4 gm | Fiber: | 4.4 gm | Zinc: | 1.4 mg |
| Iron: | 2.5 mg | Cal. from fat: | 7% | | |

# Sweet Potato Custard

• This is a luscious, creamy dessert in which the sweet potatoes are beaten into a comforting custard—perfect for finishing a meal, as a snack, or as a topping for cake. It is also a great way to use leftover sweet potatoes.

Preparation time: 10 minutes, plus 1 hour refrigeration

Cooking time: 45 minutes

Serves 4

| | |
|---|---|
| 4 medium sweet potatoes (6 ounces each) | ¼ cup orange juice, fresh or from concentrate |
| 2 tablespoons (packed) light brown sugar | 4 teaspoons fresh lemon juice |
| | ¾ cup plain low-fat yogurt |

1. Preheat oven to 400°F.

2. Bake potatoes until soft, about 45 minutes. Cool completely.

3. Remove potato pulp from skin and place in medium bowl. Add sugar and juices. Beat with electric mixer or whisk until sugar is dissolved and potatoes are light. Fold in yogurt.

4. Transfer mixture to custard cups. Refrigerate until cold, 1 hour.

### Nutrients Per Serving

| Calories: | 189 | Cholesterol: | 3 mg | Vitamin A: | 24,612 IU |
|---|---|---|---|---|---|
| Fat: | 4.4 gm | Sodium: | 50 mg | Vitamin C: | 35 mg |
| Sat. fat: | .5 gm | Fiber: | 3.7 gm | Zinc: | .7 mg |
| Iron: | .9 mg | Cal. from fat: | 21% | | |

# Raspberry-Orange Frozen Yogurt

• This creamy, smooth frozen yogurt tastes so much better than store-bought and is a lot healthier, with vitamin C throughout. You will be amazed at how easy it is to make your own frozen desserts.

Preparation time: 15 minutes

Freezing time: 5 to 6 hours

Makes 4 cups

| | |
|---|---|
| 1 cup orange juice, fresh or from concentrate | 1 package (12-ounce) frozen raspberries, without syrup, thawed (about 3 cups) |
| ¼ cup sugar | 1⅓ cups plain low-fat yogurt |
| 1 envelope gelatin | 2 teaspoons grated orange zest |

**1.** In small (1-quart) saucepan, combine juice, sugar, and gelatin. Heat over very low heat, stirring, until sugar and gelatin have dissolved. Cool to room temperature.

**2.** Add raspberries, yogurt, and zest to gelatin mixture. Whisk well to combine.

**3.** Transfer mixture to shallow metal baking pan and freeze 2 hours, then whisk again. Freeze until solid, 3 to 4 hours. Before serving, transfer mixture to food processor. Process until very smooth, about 1 minute.

### Nutrients Per Serving

| | | | | | |
|---|---|---|---|---|---|
| Calories: | 89 | Cholesterol: | 2 gm | Vitamin A: | 136 IU |
| Fat: | 1 gm | Sodium: | 29 mg | Vitamin C: | 26 mg |
| Sat. fat: | .4 gm | Fiber: | tr | Zinc: | .3 mg |
| Iron: | .5 mg | Cal. from fat: | 10% | | |

# Cantaloupe Granita

• A "granita" is an Italian fruit ice. It is not as smooth as a sorbet or sherbet. That smoothness can be attained by preparing the same mixture in an ice cream machine. This dessert will only be as sweet and flavorful as the cantaloupe that you use. Allow the fruit to fully ripen before you begin.

Preparation time: 10 minutes

Freezing time: 2 hours

Serves 4

| 1 cup water | 4 cups cantaloupe chunks |
| ¼ cup sugar | 1 tablespoon fresh lime juice |

**1.** In small (1-quart) saucepan, heat water and sugar over medium heat until dissolved. Transfer to food processor. Add cantaloupe and lime juice. Process until smooth.

**2.** Transfer mixture to shallow metal baking pan and freeze 2 hours, stirring mixture every 30 minutes. Return to food processor and process until smooth. Transfer to a covered plastic container and keep frozen until ready to serve.

## Nutrients Per Serving

| Calories: | 105 | Cholesterol: | 0 | Vitamin A: | 5,159 IU |
|---|---|---|---|---|---|
| Fat: | .4 gm | Sodium: | 15 mg | Vitamin C: | 68 mg |
| Sat. fat: | 0 | Fiber: | 1.3 gm | Zinc: | .3 mg |
| Iron: | .3 mg | Cal. from fat: 3% | | | |

# Tropical Fruit Salad

• The fruits in this salad are among the highest sources of vitamins A and C. This exotic combination will be a tantalizing surprise and a nutritious change from simple fruit salads. Be sure all the fruits are ripe so that all of their sweetness will be revealed.

Preparation time: 25 minutes

Cooking time: None

Serves 4

| | |
|---|---|
| 1 mango, peeled and cubed | 1 lime, sectioned (see note) |
| 1 cup cubed cantaloupe | ½ teaspoon grated fresh ginger |
| 1 papaya, peeled, seeded, and cubed | 1 tablespoon chopped fresh mint leaves |
| 2 kiwifruit, peeled, halved, and sliced ½ inch thick | |

In large bowl, combine mango, cantaloupe, papaya, kiwifruit, lime, ginger, and mint. Toss gently.

## Note:

To section any citrus fruit, first remove peel and pith. Using sharp paring knife, cut off top and bottom ends of fruit. Stand fruit on one flat end and run knife from top of fruit to bottom, as close to flesh as possible, cutting off peel and pith in strips. Finally, cut off any remaining pieces of pith. Holding fruit in your hand, cut out sections between membranes. Remove any seeds from sections and squeeze membranes for extra juice.

### Nutrients Per Serving

| | | | | | |
|---|---|---|---|---|---|
| Calories: | 106 | Cholesterol: | 0 | Vitamin A: | 4,935 IU |
| Fat: | .5 gm | Sodium: | 9 mg | Vitamin C: | 112 mg |
| Sat. fat: | tr | Fiber: | 2.8 gm | Zinc: | .2 mg |
| Iron: | .5 mg | Cal. from fat: 4% | | | |

# Macerated Persimmons with Lemon

• There are two varieties of persimmon readily available in America, the Hachiya and the Fuyu. When the Hachiya is ripe, its pulp is semiliquid and is often used to make puddings and breads. The Fuyu, however, remains firm and can be eaten in pieces.

Preparation time: 10 minutes

Marinating time: 2 hours

Serves 4

4 Fuyu persimmons, peeled, halved, and sliced

¼ cup fresh lemon juice

1 tablespoon sugar

1 tablespoon grated lemon zest

1 tablespoon chopped fresh mint leaves

**1.** In medium bowl, combine persimmons, juice, sugar, and zest. Cover and refrigerate 2 hours.

**2.** Sprinkle with mint just before serving.

## Nutrients Per Serving

| Calories: | 130 | Cholesterol: | 0 | Vitamin A: | 3,641 IU |
|-----------|-----|--------------|---|------------|----------|
| Fat: | tr | Sodium: | 4 mg | Vitamin C: | 38 mg |
| Sat. fat: | 0 | Fiber: | 6 gm | Zinc: | 0 |
| Iron: | .6 mg | Cal. from fat: | 1.5% | | |

**Chapter 13**

# Cookies, Cakes, and Pies

Chances are you don't need any encouragement to try recipes from the dessert category. For the most part, fresh fruits and fresh fruit salad combinations are a better routine dessert choice. Yet, when the occasion calls for something a little bit more special, the fruit desserts, bars, cake, and pie we include below are sure to fit the bill. Granted, the Carrot Spice Cake is a bit high in fat with 7 grams of fat per serving. But this is a fraction of the traditional version, and it can easily fit into a low-fat diet on those special occasions like birthdays, anniversaries, or dinner with company. With less than 5 grams of fat per serving and a hefty dose of beta-carotene, our Pumpkin Pie is a guaranteed hit for the holidays and all year round.

# Carrot Spice Cake

• Carrot cake is a classic for its great flavor. Now it can be a classic for its nutrients. Enjoy this low-fat version for dessert or as a sweet snack.

Preparation time: 20 minutes

Baking time: 1 hour 20 minutes

Serves 8

1¼ cups unbleached all-purpose flour

½ cup (packed) light brown sugar

¼ cup granulated sugar

¼ cup wheat germ

2 teaspoons baking powder

1½ teaspoons baking soda

1½ teaspoon ground cinnamon

½ teaspoon salt

¼ teaspoon ground cloves

¼ teaspoon ground allspice

3 tablespoons safflower oil

½ cup buttermilk

1 large egg

2 large egg whites

1 teaspoon pure vanilla extract

4 medium carrots, peeled and grated (3 cups)

Topping

½ cup powdered sugar

1 tablespoon milk or buttermilk

1. Preheat oven to 350°F. Spray 8x8-inch baking pan with nonstick cooking spray. Sprinkle with flour. Shake off excess.

2. In large bowl, combine flour, sugars, wheat germ, baking powder, baking soda, cinnamon, salt, cloves, and allspice. Stir well. In separate bowl, whisk together oil, buttermilk, egg, egg whites, and vanilla.

3. Pour liquid ingredients over dry. Add carrots. Stir just until blended. Pour mixture into prepared pan and bake 1 hour 20 minutes, or until toothpick inserted in center comes out clean. Cool in pan 1 hour. Remove from pan to cool completely on rack.

*continued*

**4.** In small bowl, stir together topping ingredients until smooth. With skewer, poke 1-inch holes in top of cake. Spread topping over cake. Let dry before serving, about 1 hour.

| Nutrients Per Serving | | | | | |
|---|---|---|---|---|---|
| Calories: | 309 | Cholesterol: | 27 mg | Vitamin A: | 10,334 IU |
| Fat: | 7 gm | Sodium: | 460 mg | Vitamin C: | 4.1 mg |
| Sat. fat: | 2.4 gm | Fiber: | 2.6 gm | Zinc: | 1.1 mg |
| Iron: | 2.4 mg | Cal. from fat: | 20% | | |

# Almond Angel Food Cake with Mango Puree

• Angel food cake is a decadent sweet treat for the health conscious—and everybody else. In this version, I have added almonds and all of their vitamin E to the classic cake. The real health boost, however, comes from the mango sauce, bursting with fresh flavor and beta-carotene.

Preparation time: 20 minutes

Baking time: 45 minutes

Serves 6

| | |
|---|---|
| 6 large egg whites | 1 teaspoon pure vanilla extract |
| ½ teaspoon cream of tartar | ½ teaspoon almond extract |
| ¼ teaspoon salt | ⅓ cup water |
| ½ cup plus 1 tablespoon superfine sugar | 2 tablespoons granulated sugar |
| ½ cup sifted cake flour | 3 ripe mangoes |
| ½ cup (2½ ounces) finely ground almonds | |

1. Preheat oven to 325°F.

2. In large bowl, beat egg whites until frothy. Add cream of tartar and salt; continue beating until soft peaks form. Continue beating while gradually adding superfine sugar. Beat until stiff.

3. Sift 2 tablespoons of the flour over egg whites. Gently fold into mixture. Repeat with remaining flour, 2 tablespoons at a time. Fold in nuts, then vanilla and almond extracts.

4. Transfer mixture to 9-inch tube pan. Bake until cake pulls away from sides of pan, about 45 minutes. Invert pan onto rack and cool thoroughly before removing cake.

*continued*

**5.** In small saucepan, combine water and granulated sugar. Heat until dissolved. Increase heat and boil until just beginning to color, about 6 minutes. Do not stir the syrup.

**6.** Remove mango pulp from skin and discard pit. Transfer pulp to food processor. Process until smooth. Add sugar syrup and process to mix. Serve with cake.

*Nutrients Per Serving*

| Calories: | 275 | Cholesterol: | 0 | Vitamin A: | 4,030 IU |
|-----------|-----|--------------|---|------------|----------|
| Fat: | 6 gm | Sodium: | 149 mg | Vitamin C: | 29 mg |
| Sat. fat: | .7 gm | Fiber: | 2.4 gm | Zinc: | .4 mg |
| Iron: | 1.2 mg | Cal. from fat: | 21% | | |

# Pumpkin Pie

• Pumpkin pie is thought of as a decadent treat. But now that we know how healthy pumpkin is, we need not feel guilty. With this low-fat version, we can feel virtuous.

Preparation time: 5 minutes

Baking time: 45 to 50 minutes

Serves 8

1½ cups pumpkin puree, canned or homemade

½ cup (packed) dark brown sugar

1 cup low-fat (1%) milk

2 large eggs

1 teaspoon ground cinnamon

1 teaspoon grated fresh ginger

¼ teaspoon ground allspice

1 Pie Crust (recipe below)

1. Preheat oven to 450°F.

2. In large bowl, combine pumpkin and sugar. Stir until sugar dissolves. Add milk, eggs, cinnamon, ginger, and allspice. Stir well.

3. Spoon mixture into pie crust. Bake 10 minutes. Reduce heat to 350°F and continue baking until completely set, 35 to 40 minutes. Cool on rack.

## Pie Crust

1 cup unbleached all-purpose flour

⅛ teaspoon salt

2 tablespoons chilled margarine, cut into pieces

4½ teaspoons chilled reduced-calorie margarine

2 to 3 tablespoons ice water

*continued*

1. In large bowl or food processor fitted with steel blade, combine flour and salt. Cut in margarine or pulse until mixture resembles coarse crumbs. Add water, 1 tablespoon at a time, until dough forms.

2. Press dough into ball and flatten. Wrap in plastic wrap and refrigerate 30 minutes.

3. On lightly floured surface, roll dough into an 11-inch circle. Fold in half and place in 9-inch pie plate. Proceed with pie recipe as directed.

### Nutrients Per Serving

| Calories: | 192 | Cholesterol: | 1 mg | Vitamin A: | 10,434 IU |
|-----------|-----|--------------|------|------------|-----------|
| Fat: | 5.7 gm | Sodium: | 206 mg | Vitamin C: | 2 mg |
| Sat. fat: | 1.3 gm | Fiber: | 1.2 gm | Zinc: | .4 mg |
| Iron: | 2 mg | Cal. from fat: | 27% | | |

# Apricot Squares

• These tasty bar cookies will be enjoyed by the children, but are made for grownups. They are ideal with coffee after dinner or with an afternoon cup of tea.

Preparation time: 20 minutes

Cooking time: 1 hour, including baking time

Makes 16 squares

2 cups chopped dried apricots (12 ounces)

1 cup orange juice, fresh or from concentrate

1 cup water

½ teaspoon grated fresh ginger

¾ cup unbleached all-purpose flour

¼ cup sugar

3 tablespoons wheat germ

1 teaspoon grated lemon zest

½ teaspoon salt

¼ cup cold butter, cut in small pieces

Cold water, as needed

**1.** Preheat oven to 375°F. Spray 9×9-inch baking pan with nonstick cooking spray.

**2.** In small saucepan, combine apricots, juice, water, and ginger. Cook over low heat, stirring frequently, until almost all of the moisture is absorbed, about 25 minutes.

**3.** In food processor, combine flour, sugar, wheat germ, zest, and salt. Pulse mixture until combined. Add butter and pulse until the mixture forms coarse crumbs. Add cold water, 1 teaspoon at a time, until mixture comes together.

**4.** Press dough into bottom of prepared pan. Bake 10 minutes; remove from oven. Spread apricot mixture over crust. Return to oven and bake 25 minutes. Cool completely on rack before cutting into squares.

*continued*

## Nutrients Per Serving

| | | | | | |
|---|---|---|---|---|---|
| Calories: | 122 | Cholesterol: | 8 mg | Vitamin A: | 1,660 mg |
| Fat: | 3.2 gm | Sodium: | 100 mg | Vitamin C: | 7 mg |
| Sat. fat: | 1.8 gm | Fiber: | 2 gm | Zinc: | .4 mg |
| Iron: | 1.4 mg | Cal. from fat: | 24% | | |

# Mango-Blackberry Crisp

- Vitamin A–packed mango replaces peaches in this classic fruit dessert. If blackberries are not available, replace them with raspberries or blueberries.

Preparation time: 15 minutes

Baking time: 45 minutes

Makes 6 servings

| | |
|---|---|
| 4 ripe mangoes, peeled and thinly sliced | ¼ cup (packed) light brown sugar |
| 2 cups blackberries | 3 tablespoons unbleached all-purpose flour |
| 2 tablespoons granulated sugar | ¼ teaspoon ground cinnamon |
| 2 tablespoons fresh lime juice | Pinch salt |
| ½ cup quick oats | 2 tablespoons butter, softened slightly |

1. Preheat oven to 350°F.

2. Combine mango slices, blackberries, granulated sugar, and lime juice in 8×8-inch baking pan.

3. In small bowl, combine oats, brown sugar, flour, cinnamon, and salt. Add butter, working the mixture into coarse crumbs, using fingers. Sprinkle crumbs over fruit mixture.

4. Bake until lightly browned, about 45 minutes. Serve warm or cool.

### Nutrients Per Serving

| Calories: | 241 | Cholesterol: | 11 mg | Vitamin A: | 5,557 IU |
|---|---|---|---|---|---|
| Fat: | 5.2 gm | Sodium: | 56 mg | Vitamin C: | 49 mg |
| Sat. fat: | 2.6 gm | Fiber: | 4.1 gm | Zinc: | .4 mg |
| Iron: | 1.1 mg | Cal. from fat: | 19% | | |

# Ginger-Papaya Trifle

• A touch of ginger makes this simple dessert an unusual treat. I usually serve it in neat squares from a baking pan, but it can also be beautifully arranged in a glass bowl so that the colored layers are visible.

Preparation time: 10 minutes

Refrigeration time: 4 hours

Serves 4

| | |
|---|---|
| 10 ladyfingers | 2 tablespoons sugar |
| 1 tablespoon fresh lemon juice | 1 papaya, peeled and sliced |
| 2 cups plain low-fat yogurt | 1 pint strawberries, sliced |
| 2 tablespoons minced fresh ginger | |

**1.** Arrange ladyfingers to cover bottom of an 8x8-inch baking pan. Sprinkle ladyfingers with lemon juice.

**2.** In small bowl, combine the yogurt, ginger, and sugar. Stir well.

**3.** Spread half of yogurt mixture evenly over ladyfingers. Arrange the papaya slices over yogurt. Cover papaya with remaining yogurt mixture. Top with strawberry slices.

**4.** Cover pan with plastic wrap and refrigerate 4 hours before serving. Cut in slices to serve.

### Nutrients Per Serving

| Calories: | 253 | Cholesterol: | 107 mg | Vitamin A: | 1,781 IU |
|---|---|---|---|---|---|
| Fat: | 4.7 gm | Sodium: | 124 mg | Vitamin C: | 95 mg |
| Sat. fat: | 1.9 gm | Fiber: | 2.8 gm | Zinc: | 1.5 mg |
| Iron: | 1.5 mg | Cal. from fat: | 17% | | |

# Liquid and Dry Measure Equivalencies

| CUSTOMARY | METRIC |
|---|---|
| 1/4 teaspoon | 1.25 milliliters |
| 1/2 teaspoon | 2.5 milliliters |
| 1 teaspoon | 5 milliliters |
| 1 tablespoon | 15 milliliters |
| 1 fluid ounce | 30 milliliters |
| 1/4 cup | 60 milliliters |

*Liquid and Dry Measure Equivalencies (continued)*

| CUSTOMARY | METRIC |
|---|---|
| 1/3 cup | 80 milliliters |
| 1/2 cup | 120 milliliters |
| 1 cup | 240 milliliters |
| 1 pint (2 cups) | 480 milliliters |
| 1 quart (4 cups; 32 ounces) | 960 milliliters (.96 liter) |
| 1 gallon (4 quarts) | 3.84 liters |
| 1 ounce (by weight) | 28 grams |
| 1/4 pound (4 ounces) | 114 grams |
| 1 pound (16 ounces) | 454 grams |
| 2.2 pounds | 1 kilogram (1,000 grams) |

*Oven Temperature Equivalents*

| DESCRIPTION | °FAHRENHEIT | °CELSIUS |
|---|---|---|
| Cool | 200 | 90 |
| Very slow | 250 | 120 |
| Slow | 300–325 | 150–160 |
| Moderately slow | 325–350 | 160–180 |
| Moderate | 350–375 | 180–190 |
| Moderately hot | 375–400 | 190–200 |
| Hot | 400–450 | 200–230 |
| Very hot | 450–500 | 230–260 |

# General Index

(For recipes, *see* Index of Recipes which follows.)

abbreviation table, 42
aging, 13, 15, 32, 34
Agriculture Department, U.S., 21
air pollution, 14
almonds, 30
Alzheimer's, 14, 18–19
amaranth, 28
anemia, Fanconi's, 19
antioxidants, 13–19
  aging and, 13, 15
  building diet rich in, 21–35
  cancer and, 13, 16–17, 18, 23, 25
  cataracts and, 17, 23, 25
  free-radical reactions squelched by, 14
  heart disease and, 13, 17–18, 23, 25, 29
  immune system and, 13, 15–16, 23, 29
  seven-day menu plan rich in, 37–41
  *see also specific antioxidants*
apigenin, 35
apples, 13, 35
apricots, 25, 31
arteriosclerosis, 14
arthritis, 14, 19
artichokes, 29
asparagus, 28, 31
avocadoes, 25, 29, 30

beans, 33, 34
beef, 33
beet greens, 25, 28
beta-carotene, 13, 14, 15–16, 22–25
  cancer and, 16, 23
  cataracts and, 17, 23
  foods containing, 24–25
  heart disease and, 18, 23
  nutrient conservation tips for, 23–24

  protective dose of, 23
  toxicity problems with, 23
black beans, 34
blackberries, 28
black-eyed peas, 34
bladder cancer, 17
Bloom syndrome, 19
blueberries, 28
breakfast, 22
breast cancer, 23
broccoli, 13, 18, 22, 23, 25, 26, 27, 34, 35
brussels sprouts, 27, 34
butternut squash, 24

cabbage, 24, 26, 28, 34
cancer, 13, 14, 16–17, 18, 23, 25, 31, 34–35
cantaloupe, 23, 24, 26, 27
carambolas, 28
carcinogens, 16
carrots, 18, 23, 24
cataracts, 14, 17, 23, 25, 29
cauliflower, 28
cervical cancer, 17
cherimoyas, 27
chicken, 33, 34
chickpeas, 33
cholesterol:
  HDL, 18
  LDL, 14, 18, 35
cigarette smoke, 14
citrus fruits, 18
clams, 33
cold (common), 25
collards, 24, 28
colon cancer, 17
cooking:
  beta-carotene and, 23
  vitamin C and, 26
  vitamin E and, 29–30
  zinc and, 33
corn oil, 31
cottonseed oil, 30
cranberries, 29
cruciferous vegetables, 13, 34–35
  *see also specific vegetables*

diabetes mellitus, 14, 19
DNA, 14, 16, 18
dry measure equivalencies, 215

esophageal cancer, 17
eye ailments, 14, 17, 23, 25, 29

Fanconi's anemia, 19
flavonoids, 13, 15, 35
Food and Nutrition Board, 31
Food Guide Pyramid, 38
free radicals, 14–19
  aging and, 13, 15
  Alzheimer's and, 14, 18–19
  cancer and, 14, 16–17
  cataracts and, 14, 17
  damaging effects of, 14
  defined, 14
  heart disease and, 14, 17–18
  immune function and, 14, 15–16
  sources of, 14
fruits:
  beta-carotene sources, 24–25
  conserving nutrients in, 23–24, 26, 29–30, 32, 33
  daily servings of, 17
  vitamin C sources, 27–29
  vitamin E sources, 30–31
  *see also specific fruits*

garbanzo beans, 33
genetic disorders, 14, 19
glutathione, 15
gooseberries, 28
grapefruit juice, 27
greens, 24, 25, 28, 31
guavas, 27

Harvard Medical School, 18
hazelnuts, 30
HDL cholesterol, 18
heart attack, 18
heart disease, 13, 14, 17–18, 23, 25, 29, 31, 35
"helper" T-lymphocytes, 15
HIV, 15
hominy, 34

honeydew melons, 28
Human Nutrition Research Center on Aging, 17
Huntington's chorea, 14, 19
hypertension, 14, 19

immune system, 13, 14, 15–16, 23, 29, 31, 32
indoles, 13, 15, 34–35
infections, 25

Johns Hopkins Medical Institute, 35

kaempherol, 35
kale, 25, 28
kidney beans, 34
kiwifruit, 27
kohlrabi, 27

larynx cancer, 17
LDL cholesterol, 14, 18, 35
lentils, 34
lima beans, 34
liquid measure equivalencies, 215
lung cancer, 16–17, 23
luteolin, 35

macular degeneration, 14, 17, 29
Mandarin oranges, 27
mangoes, 24, 27, 30
margarine, 30
meat, 33
menu plan, seven-day antioxidant-rich, 37–41
mitochondria, 18
mustard greens, 25, 28, 31
mutations, 14, 18
myricetin, 35

National Academy of Sciences, 31
National Cancer Institute, 17, 23
natural killer (NK) cells, 15, 31
nerve cells, 18
nuts, 30

oils, 30, 31
onions, 35
orange juice, 27
oranges, 27
osteoarthritis, 14, 19
oysters, 33
ozone, 14

pancreatic cancer, 17
papayas, 24, 27

Parkinson's disease, 14
parsley, 25, 28
peanut butter, 30
peanuts, 30
peas, split, 34
peppers, 27
persimmons, 25, 28
Physicians' Health Study, 18
pineapple, 28
pineapple juice, 28
pinto beans, 34
pollution, 14
potatoes, 26
preeclampsia, 14, 19
pumpkin, 18, 24

quercetin, 35

radishes, 29
raspberries, 28
Recommended Dietary Allowances (RDAs), 23, 25, 29, 32
rectal cancer, 17
restaurants, eating in, 22

safflower oil, 30
salmon, 34
seafood, 32, 33, 34
seeds, 30
selenium, 13, 14, 15, 22, 31–32
    foods containing, 31
    nutrient conservation tips for, 32
    protective dose of, 32
    toxicity problems with, 32
seven-day antioxidant-rich menu plan, 37–41
shrimp, 34
snow peas, 28
spinach, 18, 22, 24, 26, 28, 31, 34
squash, winter, 24, 25
squid, 34
stomach cancer, 17
strawberries, 27
stroke, 18
sulforophane, 13, 35
sunflower seeds, 30
supplements, 16
    beta-carotene, 15–16
    selenium, 32
    vitamin C, 26
    vitamin E, 18, 30, 31
    zinc, 32
sweet potatoes, 24, 28, 30
swordfish, 34

systemic lupus erythematosis (SLE), 19

tea, 35
T-lymphocytes, 15, 31
tomatoes, 26, 28
tomato paste, 27
trout, rainbow, 34
Tufts University, 18
tumors, 31
tuna, 34
turnip greens, 24, 31

ultraviolet (UV-A) radiation, 16, 17

veal, 33
vegetable oils, 30
vegetables:
    beta-carotene sources, 24–25
    conserving nutrients in, 23–24, 26, 29–30, 32, 33
    cruciferous, 13, 34–35
    daily servings of, 17
    vitamin C sources, 27–29
    vitamin E sources, 30–31
    zinc sources, 33–34
    see also specific vegetables
vitamin A, 22, 23
vitamin C, 13, 14, 15, 22, 25–29
    cataracts and, 17, 25
    foods containing, 27–29
    heart disease and, 18, 25
    nutrient conservation tips for, 26
    protective dose of, 25
    toxicity problems with, 25–26
vitamin E, 13, 14, 15, 16, 22, 29–31
    foods containing, 30–31
    heart disease and, 18, 29
    nutrient conservation tips for, 29–30
    protective dose of, 29
    toxicity problems with, 29

walnuts, 31
wheat germ, 30
Wilmer Eye Institute, 17
wine, 35

zinc, 15, 32–34
    foods containing, 33–34
    nutrient conservation tips for, 33
    protective dose of, 32
    toxicity problems with, 32

# Recipe Index

spinach (cont.)
 spread, 51
 veal, and Provençal herb
  lasagne, 135–36
spreads:
 Provençal tuna, 50
 spinach, 51
squash:
 butternut, and orange soup, 89
 butternut, puree of roasted
  garlic and, 161
 pumpkin-nut quick bread,
  72–73
 pumpkin pie, 209–10
steak, sliced, and roasted tomato
 salad, 143–44
stew, Moroccan lamb and vegetable, 131–32
stir-fry, simple vegetable,
 159
strawberry:
 mango shake, 74
 soup, cold, with balsamic
  vinegar, 92
summer tomato salad, 187
sweet potato:
 custard, 198
 fries, baked, 160
 rosemary salad, 186
 topping, shepherd's pie with,
  133–34
swordfish, grilled, with mango
 salsa, 122–23
syrup, mango maple, 63–64

tabouli, 190–91
terrine, layered roasted vegetable, 95–96
tomato(es):
 and avocado salsa, 59–60
 cabbage soup, rich, 79
 caper dressing, chicory salad
  with, 188
 crostini, 56
 double-, herb sauce, penne
  with, 109–10

fettucine with chicken, basil and,
 137–38
layered roasted vegetable terrine,
 95–96
orange salsa, beefsteak with, 128
roasted, and sliced steak salad,
 143–44
roasted, orecchiete with wilted
 greens and, 107–8
roasting, 107
saffron paella with artichokes,
 red peppers and, 103–4
salad, summer, 187
sauce, spicy, fish cooked in,
 126–27
soup, spicy summer, 91
-stuffed pork tenderloin with
 roasted poblano sauce, 129–30
trifle, ginger papaya, 214
tropical:
 citrus shake, 75
 fruit salad, 201
tuna:
 salad, ginger-marinated, 47
 salad composé, 151–52
 spread, Provençal, 50
turnip-potato puree, 169
tzimmes, carrot and prune, 162

veal, spinach, and Provençal herb
 lasagne, 135–36
vegetable(s):
 brown rice with almonds and,
  171–72
 and lamb stew, Moroccan,
  131–32
 marinated, 54–55
 stir-fry, simple, 159
 see also side dishes; specific vegetables
vegetable main dishes, 93–115
 barley-stuffed cabbage with red
  pepper sauce, 97–98
 carrot and broccoli risotto, 114–15
 carrot and chickpea curry, 101–2
 fettucine with tomatoes and
  basil, 137

fusilli with roasted vegetables,
 105–6
layered roasted vegetable terrine,
 95–96
orecchiete with wilted greens
 and roasted tomatoes, 107–8
penne with double-tomato herb
 sauce, 109–10
potato-kale frittata, 99–100
red and green pepper lasagne,
 112–13
saffron paella with artichokes,
 tomatoes, and red peppers,
 103–4
spaghetti with spinach ricotta
 and basil, 111
vegetable stir-fry with brown
 rice, 159
vinaigrette:
 asparagus salad, 182
 fresh raspberry, 177

walnut-raspberry muffins, 68–69
watercress salad with oranges and
 grapefruit, 189
wheatberry:
 cereal, hot, 67
 sauté, 173–74
white bean-parsley dip, 48
whole-wheat garlic chips, 52–53
wild rice:
 chicken salad with mango and
  ginger, 154–55
 with oranges and scallions, 170

yogurt:
 ginger papaya trifle, 214
 raspberry-orange frozen, 199
 strawberry-mango shake, 74

zucchini, in layered roasted vegetable terrine, 95–96